BIG PICTURE PEOPLE

My friend Doug Carter seems to have pulled up a chair by a warm, inviting fireplace or his favorite boyhood fishing hole to chat with friends. In a real and candid way, Doug shares with us his wisdom about leadership principles that have formed and shaped his life and ministry. He combines humor, Scripture, experience, scholarship, and plain old south Georgia charm and common sense to teach us the joy of living as *Big Picture People*.

—William E. Flippin
Senior pastor, Greater Piney Grove Baptist Church
Atlanta

I have known Doug Carter since he was a small lad. I was in attendance at the camp meeting service when he and his wife, Winnie, answered God's call to Christian service, and I have followed along every step of their spiritual journey. I highly recommend *Big Picture People*. The content is challenging, inspiring, and spiritually helpful—plus it is very easy to read.

—Mrs. George E. Luce
Fort Valley, Georgia

Doug Carter is my spiritual and leadership mentor. No one has taught me more about life and leadership than Doug. When I was a college student, he took me under his wing and began to teach me by admonition and example the principles you will discover in his book *Big Picture People*. This book *is* Doug Carter. I'm confident that the principles in this book will impact your life as profoundly as they have mine.

—Bret Layton
Senior pastor, Elk River Church of the Nazarene
Charleston, West Virginia

It has been my privilege for nearly 30 years to call Doug Carter my friend. I've walked with him through both wonderful and difficult days; however, through it all he has proved himself to be a man of integrity and principle. His book gives insight into the things God uses to make a man of character and courage—a man like Doug Carter. In the years ahead I will refer often to this outstanding volume.

—David Dean
Senior pastor, Brookside Church
Chillicothe, Ohio

Here's a book that will stir your heart and sharpen your faith. As a leader of leaders, Doug Carter has consistently lived out the timeless principles he shares with us in *Big Picture People*. You're sure to enjoy this book and refer to it regularly.

—Jim Dorsey
Senior pastor, The Family Church
Rancho Santa Margarita, California

How refreshing to read a real-life story of success! Through tears and triumphs, from experience and by example, Doug Carter opens the door of his life and shows us how maximum dependence upon God always produces maximum victory in Jesus.

—David A. Gallimore
Senior pastor, Metro West Church of the Nazarene
Orlando, Florida

BIG PICTURE PEOPLE

Overcoming
a Knothole
View
of
Life

DOUG CARTER

Beacon Hill Press of Kansas City
Kansas City, Missouri

ISBN 083-411-7991

Printed in the
United States of America

Cover Design: Kevin Williamson

Front Cover Photo Courtesy of National Aeronautics and
Space Administration

Library of Congress Cataloging-in-Publication Data

Carter, Doug, 1941-
  Big picture people : overcoming a knothole view of life / Doug
    Carter.
    p. cm.
  Includes bibliographical references (p.).
  ISBN 0-8341-1799-1 (pb)
    1. Christian life—Church of the Nazarene authors. 2. Carter, Doug,
  1941- I. Title.

  BV4501.2.C2725 2000
  248.4'8799—dc21

                          00-037869

10   9   8   7   6   5   4   3   2   1

To Winnie, my loving companion and best friend.

To Angie, Eric, and Jason, our three children, who have wonderfully enriched my life.

To the memory of my parents, Floyd and Vera Carter, who now reside in the heavenly city.

To my brother, James, who taught me the value of hard work.

To my sister Marguerite, whose Christ-centered life challenged me to totally surrender to Him;

And to my sisters Mary Kathryn and Johnnie, who proved to me that Christians can live victoriously in difficult times.

Acknowledgments

To Stan Toler, Dan Schafer, Shelly McCollum, and Anita Bosworth, who have given invaluable assistance and encouragement throughout this project. They have proven that true friendship is more valuable than diamonds and more to be desired than all the wealth of the world.

To Kelly Gallagher and Beacon Hill Press of Kansas City for their support and belief in these words.

To Debbie Goodwin for investing her talents in this project. It was her creativity and hard work that kept me focused on the big picture when the finish line seemed impossible to reach. I appreciate you, Debbie.

Contents

Introduction

"Do you want to catch a big one?" he asked.

My eight-year-old eyes danced with excitement and anticipation as I replied, "Yes, sir!"

Soon my dad and I began an adventure from which I learned countless important lessons about the big picture.

We were on one of our all-too-seldom fishing trips, if you can call it a trip when you're only about two miles from home. The day began early, grubbing for earthworms. This involved rubbing a red brick across a short stake we had pounded into the ground in an area populated with tall, stately pine trees. After filling a small can with a handful of black soil and the earthworms we roused, we climbed into the car. Our two cane poles extended from an open window and waved in the breeze. As the old Ford rattled down the unpaved country road, our neighbor waved and yelled, "Good luck!"

We turned off the main road and rambled several hundred yards through the woods, creating a new road as we bumped along. Dad said, "We'll have to walk from here." Knowing that it would be my task to carry the can of worms and the cane poles through the deep woods, I muttered under my breath, "I sure hope the fishing hole isn't far away."

My dad muttered nothing, although this trek through the woods would be extremely difficult for him because of his crippling arthritis. His doctors had warned him that his bones had been damaged by the arthritis and were prone to break easily. I did wonder what would happen if my dad fell. Even though I was rather large for an eight-year-old, I knew I would be helpless to lift my dad if he stumbled and fell.

Finally we arrived at the fishing hole, a rather deep lake through which flowed a creek. Tangled lines were the only problem we had encountered from our trek through the bushes and tree limbs. I suppose I shouldn't have used the poles for machetes in clearing a path through the woods.

We had fished for several hours and caught nothing when my dad asked again, "Do you want to catch a big one?" Frankly, I would have been happy to catch any-thing—even a minnow!

However, thoughts of "a big one" overpowered me, and I replied, "Yes, sir."

Instead of changing bait or divulging some other fish-ing strategy, he told me we would have to change our place. "Several hundred yards beyond us, through some deep woods filled with thorns and briars, is a much larger lake," said Dad. "It's full of big ones, but there's no easy way to get there." He grinned when he added, "We'll have to cross the creek on a footlog and force our way through the briars." The prospect of bloody cuts from the briars didn't concern me as much as the thought of my crippled dad trying to walk across a creek on a footlog.

The footlog was a small, fallen pine tree that bridged the distance from one creek bank to the other. I didn't be-lieve that my dad, even with the help of his cane, could safely cross the creek. I could see him toppling into the muddy water while all my rescue efforts failed. Fear seized me.

I opened my mouth to try to convince Dad of the risks when he exclaimed, "Nothing ventured, nothing gained!" He handed me the worm can and the poles and said, "Fear destroys dreams. Your dream of the big one can come true if you will go where other people are afraid to go." He placed his hand on my shoulder, whispered a short prayer asking God to protect us, and said, "Walk slowly, don't look down, keep your eyes fixed on the other side of the creek, and whatever you do—don't spill the bait!"

Following my father's unbelievable footwork, we

crossed the footlog without a problem. Then we pushed through a jungle of underbrush to reach the banks of the larger fishing hole. My hook had hardly touched water when the cork bobbed and disappeared. I gave a mighty heave and launched a huge fish into the hot, humid air of a summer afternoon in southern Georgia. The fish landed behind me in the brush and fluttered wildly. I pounced and shouted, "I've got a big one!"

I had no way of knowing that less than two years later my father would say good-bye to his family and enter his heavenly home. However, the lessons of the fishing hole from that day and others continue to teach me. They're lessons about life and leadership. They're lessons that emphasize the *big picture*.

Through the years many other devout men and women have helped to shape my life. This book is my attempt to share some of the principles and values they have taught me. They are precepts that have guided me as a husband, father, missionary, evangelist, college president, elected official, and mission executive. They are principles that keep me focused on the *big picture*. My prayer is that they will do the same for you.

The future belongs to those
who see possibilities
before they become obvious.
—John Sculley

We live by faith, not by sight.
—2 Cor. 5:7

1

Knotholes

Looking at life through a knothole is not the big picture.

There once was a young boy who dreamed of the day when he could see circus animals on parade. One day he learned that a circus train would stop in a nearby town and that the animals would walk down Main Street to the large tent. After walking miles, the youngster discovered the streets were so crowded that there was no place to get a good view. The only place to stand was along a tall wood fence bordering the street. His dream of seeing exotic jungle beasts evaporated. Running along the fence, he found a small knothole. He knelt down and peered through the small hole—only to be overcome with further disappointment. Through the knothole he could see only the legs of giraffes, zebras, and elephants. He dropped his head and began the long walk home.

A gentleman standing nearby observed the lad's dilemma. He made his way to the boy, placed his hands under the boy's arms, and lifted him high above the fence. Now the youngster could see the big picture. What a panorama! As he gazed from one end of the street to the other, his heart celebrated. The animals were more beautiful than he had ever imagined.

How desperately we need to see the big picture! Too often we live with "knothole views" of God and His plan. We substitute our problems and difficult circumstances for the big picture. If only we could see the greatness of our God, the vastness of His resources, and how much He desires to involve us in His great rescue plan for lost men and women around the world. How desperately we need to be "big picture people"!

Knothole views seem to be an occupational hazard of the human race. Numerous examples of people who could not see the big picture abound in the Bible. Thankfully, there are many examples of "big picture people" as well.

Lot's Knothole View

Clearly, Lot had a knothole view of life. He could see only the here and now. Like many today who are obsessed with gadgets, toys, pleasures, and other playthings, Lot could see only the temporal. Consequently, he "pitched his tent toward Sodom" (Gen. 13:9-12, KJV).

What you see and hear depends a
good deal on where you
are standing; it also depends on
what sort of person you are.
—C. S. Lewis

Abraham Was a Big Picture Person

Abraham gave Lot the first choice. He was willing to take leftovers after Lot selected his land. Abraham had caught the big picture, the eternal vista. How could he spend his life obsessed with goats, sheep, camels, servants, and watering holes when he had discovered God's plan to redeem planet Earth? God had promised him a son and a family. Through his family would come the Messiah and the Church. Through the Church the message of salvation would go to the ends of the earth. Abraham was part of an eternal promise. He was involved in something *big!* Through him and his descendants the whole world would be blessed (Gen. 12:1-3).

> Don't put your hope into things that
> change—relationships, money, talents,
> beauty, even health. Set your sights on the
> one thing that can never change:
> trust in your Heavenly Father.
> —Max Lucado

Haggai and a Knothole Gang

In the little Book of Haggai, the children of Israel have returned from exile. God speaks through the prophet and instructs them to rebuild the Temple. Immediately they commence work on the Temple, but the "knothole gang" stands nearby to discourage the workers. They say the job is too big, the resources are too small, and whatever they build will never be as beautiful or magnificent as what King Solomon built.

The laborers are ready to quit when God speaks through the prophet again. He reminds them that He is their colaborer (2:4), that He has unlimited resources (v. 8), and that He will fill the restored Temple with His glory, making it good enough (vv. 7, 9).

> If you're looking for a big opportunity,
> seek out a big problem.

Joseph Looked Beyond the Knothole

Joseph could easily have lived at the knothole. After all, his life consisted of one tragedy after another. He lived from pit to pit to pit, but he never let the pit get into him. He lost coat after coat after coat, but he never lost his integrity. Whether in the pit of rejection, the pit of temptation, or the pit of injustice, he always looked beyond difficult circumstances and saw God in control and working

The Big Picture Frame

Big picture people

refuse to allow

present circumstances

to blind them.

They live with eternity in view.

out His plan. His years of faithfulness paid off—he became second in command in Egypt, where God used him to deliver His people from starvation during the great famine.

How did Joseph maintain his big picture focus on God during extremely difficult and painful circumstances? How did he remain positive in a negative world?

He did not despise the hard places.

His faith increased as he experienced God's sustaining grace in crisis after crisis. He learned the discipline of work, of self-control. And of suffering.

He did not base his relationship with God on his emotions.

He knew that emotions are neither a cause nor a measure of spirituality.

He knew that everything minus integrity equals zero.

He resisted temptation and refused to sin against God.

He was not bound by the past.

He refused to spend his life gazing into the rearview mirror. He allowed God to heal the hurts that others had inflicted upon him.

Trials are only blessings in disguise.
—John Wesley

Nick Refused Knothole Views

In October 1996 while I was in Evansville, Indiana, to preach revival services, a friend asked me to go with him to visit a 25-year-old quadriplegic. The young man had suffered paralysis from the neck down in a terrible car accident 8 years before. When I walked into the living room and saw the young man sitting motionless in his motorized wheelchair, I could hardly believe that he was once a high school star football running back who could run 40 yards in 4.5 seconds.

After he greeted me, he began to tell me that Jesus had forgiven his sins and transformed his life. He said with a smile, "I'm so richly blessed and so thankful for God's wonderful grace." He quickly added, "When I was strong and could run like the wind, I was self-centered, self-sufficient, and didn't need God; but the accident brought me face-to-face with my need for God." With a joyful grin he added, "The old Nick is gone—I'm now a new creation in Christ. He fills my heart with joy."

The same God that guided His Son
through death and back to life said He will
never leave or forsake us. He is right
there with you, perhaps even more in times
of crisis than any other time.
—Max Lucado

With the radiant joy of Christ shining from his face, he explained, "I'll walk again someday, maybe in this life—but certainly in the next!" In my mind I could see him leaping down the streets of gold in the New

Jerusalem. There won't be any wheelchairs in heaven.

Then he made a statement I'll never forget. Speaking slowly but with certainty, he said, "If walking again in this life would lead to me to be self-sufficient again and cause me to drift away from God, then I'd earnestly pray that He would leave me as I am. I have peace and joy in my heart, the Holy Spirit to comfort and guide me, and the promise of eternity with my Savior—so really, how could I ask for more?"

J thank God for my handicaps, for through them J have found myself, my work, and my God.
—Helen Keller

As I left his room that day, I witnessed a far greater miracle than physical healing. I saw a young man living victoriously in the middle of what looked like tragedy. I saw a young man who focused on God, not on his circumstances. I witnessed faith accepting a situation that will not make sense until the day when we see circumstances in reverse. I saw faith embracing God's promises with such resolve that it could relinquish the present questions for the sake of future answers.

God intends troubles should be the nursery of virtue, the exercise of wisdom, the trial of patience, the venturing for a crown, and the gate of glory.
—John Wesley

Knotholes offer limited perspectives that bring discouragement and defeat. The big picture requires a perspective that only the Holy Spirit can provide. Let the Holy Spirit lift you above the fences that limit your vision of God. Let Him lift you above circumstances that confuse. Let Him help you find your place in His big picture. Let Him show you *who* makes the difference.

Action Points

- ✓ Where have I allowed a knothole view of my life to restrict my understanding of God and His big picture?
- ✓ Do I have a knothole gang who prevent me from seeing the big picture?
- ✓ Have I misused difficult circumstances in ways that blind me from a big picture view?
- ✓ Do I know how to move away from the knothole?

Think About It

Your attitude is either your best friend or your worst enemy, your greatest asset or your greatest enemy.

—John Maxwell

In learning to depend on God,
we must accept that we do not
know all the answers, but we know
who knows all the answers.
—Max Lucado

He is before all things,
and in him all things hold together.
—Col. 1:17

2

Knowing Who

*The content is more important than
the extent of knowledge.*

Far too many people focus on questions of secondary importance. We want to know the why, where, when, what, and how answers to life questions. But the who question is the all-important one. It's the *big question*.

No one can solve all the mysteries or answer every question. Attempting to be an expert on everything is an endless journey. Besides, it keeps you from seeing the big picture.

When Paul answered the who question, he saw the big picture.

Jesus confronted Paul on the Damascus road. Paul asked, "Who are you, Lord?" (Acts 9:5). When Jesus answered him, Paul responded with faith and obedience. Later Paul would write, "I know whom I have believed" (2 Tim. 1:12).

Settle the *who* question first. Then trust Him with all the other questions. When we focus on Jesus and make Him the center of our lives, we discover that the all-powerful, never-failing, totally sufficient, ever present Christ is willing and able to take us victoriously through every situation of life—even through those times when there are no answers to the why, where, when, what, and how questions. He becomes the only answer we need. Like Paul, we exclaim triumphantly, "In him we live and move and have our being" (Acts 17:28).

The Big Picture Frame

Big picture people
see Jesus as the all-sufficient Christ
revealed in Scripture.
They view life through His eyes first.

Q: Where do we get the big picture?
A: From the Artist.

JESUS IS . . .

Abel's offering . . . Noah's ark . . . Abraham's promise
. . . Jacob's ladder . . . Joseph's dream . . . Moses' rod . . .
Joshua's courage . . . Samson's strength . . . David's sling
. . . Solomon's wisdom . . . Isaiah's Messiah . . . Ezekiel's
vision . . . Jeremiah's compassion . . . Daniel's protection
. . . Elijah's chariot . . . Elisha's mantle . . . Ruth's Redeemer . . . Esther's obedience . . . Gideon's army . . . Nehemiah's commitment . . . Bartimaeus's sight . . . Zacchaeus's
forgiveness . . . Paul's gospel . . . John's revelation . . . alto-
gether lovely to the artist . . . the Bright and Morning Star
to the astronaut . . . the Bread of Life to the baker . . . un-
searchable Riches to the banker . . . the Rose of Sharon to
the botanist . . . the Chief Cornerstone to the builder . . .
the Prince of Peace to the diplomat . . . the Great Physi-
cian to the doctor . . . the Seed to the farmer . . . the True
Vine to the gardener . . . the Rock of Ages to the geologist
. . . the Pearl of Great Price to the jeweler . . . the Faithful
Witness to the judge . . . the Chief Advocate to the lawyer
. . . the Lawgiver to the legislator . . . the Song of Redemption to the musician . . . the Way, the Truth, and the Life
to the philosopher . . . glorious freedom to the prisoner

. . . the Chief Counselor to the psychologist . . . good tidings of great joy to the reporter . . . the Beginning of all things to the scientist . . . healing to the sick . . . the Captain of our salvation to the soldier . . . the Desire of all nations to the statesman . . . the Truth to the teacher . . . the Alpha and Omega to the writer . . . the Lamb of God to the zoologist . . . the Light to the blind . . . the Way to the lost . . . rest to the weary . . . joy unspeakable to the discouraged . . . the Savior to the sinner . . . and returning King to the expectant Christian.

THE BIG PICTURE BOOK

In Genesis, Jesus is the Creator God. • In Exodus, the Passover Lamb. • In Leviticus, the sin offering. • In Numbers, the brazen serpent. • In Deuteronomy, the great Lawgiver. • In Joshua, the mighty Conqueror. • In Judges, the longsuffering God. • In Ruth, our kinsman Redeemer. • In 1 Samuel, the Anointed One. • In 2 Samuel, the King of Israel. • In 1 Kings, the God who answers by fire. • In 2 Kings, the double portion. • In 1 Chronicles, the sovereign God. • In 2 Chronicles, the glory of the Lord. • In Ezra, the word of the Lord. • In Nehemiah, the Builder. • In Esther, the salvation of His people. • In Job, the Redeemer who lives. • In Psalms, the Good Shepherd. • In Proverbs, the All-wise One. • In Ecclesiastes, the true riches. • In the Song of Solomon, the Lover of our souls. • In Isaiah, the Prince of Peace. • In Jeremiah, the Master Potter. • In Lamentations, the Man of sorrows. • In Ezekiel, the River of Life. • In Daniel, the fourth Man in the fire. • In Hosea, the faithful Husband. • In Joel, the rain of the Spirit. • In Amos, the Man of humility. • In Obadiah, the wrath of God. • In Jonah, the mercy of the Lord. • In Micah, the promised Messiah. • In Nahum, a stronghold in time of trouble. • In Habakkuk, the God of my salvation. • In Zephaniah, the sword of the Lord. • In Haggai, the Desire of all nations. • In Zechariah, the Fountain opened for sin. • In Malachi, the Sun of Righteousness with healing in His wings. • In Matthew, the kingly Messiah. • In Mark, the servant Messiah. • In Luke, the Son of Man. • In John, the Son of God. • In Acts, the Head of the Church. • In Romans, the power of God unto salvation. • In 1 Corinthians, the more excellent way. • In 2 Corinthians, God's unspeakable Gift. • In Galatians, the grace of God. • In Ephesians, the Chief Cornerstone. • In Philippians, the peace of God that passes all understanding. • In Colossians, the hope of glory. • In 1 Thessalonians, our sanctification. • In 2 Thessalonians, our peace. • In 1 Timothy, the Mediator between God and man. • In 2 Timothy, the One able to keep that which I have committed unto Him. • In Titus, our blessed hope. • In Philemon, a brother beloved. • In Hebrews, our great High Priest. • In James, the crown of life. • In 1 Peter, the Lamb without spot or blemish. • In 2 Peter, our precious promises. • In 1 John, the propitiation for our sins. • In 2 John, love. • In 3 John, the Truth. • In Jude, the One able to keep us from falling. • In Revelation, the King of Kings and Lord of Lords! •

ANOTHER PICTURE

Jesus was 100 percent God and 100 percent man.
He was unique in His
    virgin birth
        virtuous life
            vicarious death
                victorious resurrection
                visible return.

The Bible was provided for us as a vehicle to carry us so that we might see Jesus Christ.
—Max Lucado

God answered "Who"
forever!

Picture This

The religious leaders of Israel quizzed Jesus when He visited the Temple in Jerusalem at age 12 (Luke 2:46-47). If they asked Jesus who He was, He might have answered this way:

Q: What is Your name?

A: On My mother's side My name is Jesus. **On My Father's side My name is King of Kings and Lord of Lords.**

Q: How old are You?

A: On My mother's side I am 12 years old. **On My Father's side I am from eternity to eternity.**

Q: Just who are You?

A: On My mother's side I am a carpenter boy. **On My Father's side I am the Way, the Truth, and the Life.**

Q: Where is Your home?

A: On My mother's side I am from Nazareth of Galilee.

On My Father's side I am from the right hand of the throne of God.

Q: What does Your future hold?

A: On My mother's side, death on an old rugged cross.

On My Father's side, victory over death, hell, and the grave; eternal power and glory; a kingdom that will never end. Hallelujah!

The Wrong Picture

Anyone who neglects to study the Holy Bible will most likely hold an inadequate understanding of Christ and may even develop an inaccurate view. A person who fails to see Jesus as He is revealed in the Scriptures is at risk of slowly fashioning for himself or herself a nonscriptural Jesus.

The modern Jesus whom some people have designed for themselves is the ultimate enemy of the Jesus revealed in the Bible. Two characteristics mark the nonbiblical Jesus designed by human hands: (1) A nonbiblical Jesus condones sin in our lives. (2) A nonbiblical Jesus lowers the cost of discipleship.

The biblical Christ never condones sin. He confronts, convicts, and converts. He forgives and transforms. Then He says, "Go now and leave your life of sin" (John 8:11).

If you desire to become more like Jesus, if you want to get closer and know Him better, then be prepared to have Him uproot sin from your life.
—Joni Eareckson Tada

The Big Picture Is the Real Picture

The Christ of the Bible insists on first place in the lives of His disciples. He demands an unconditional surrender to His Lordship and full commitment to His will (see Luke 9:23-24).

When God measures a person,
He puts the tape around the heart
instead of the head.

In this age of outlet malls and flea markets, everyone is searching for a discount. It seems to me that most Christians want a discounted discipleship. Is it possible that we desire a crown without the Cross? Do we want to reign and rule with Christ but refuse to be crucified with Him? Do we insist on the glory without any suffering?

There are no victories at bargain prices.
—Dwight D. Eisenhower

Close Enough?

One man asked another, "Which is worse—ignorance or apathy?"

The other replied, "I don't know, and I don't care."

An attitude of complacency and indifference seems to grip many Christians today. I'm reminded of the elderly widow lady who planned to marry a man she had known for only a few days. Her best friend suggested to her that the gentleman was interested only in her money. The elderly lady said to her fiancé, "Could you bring me proof you have $100,000 in the bank?" After several weeks she asked, "How are you doing on the $100,000?" He replied, "I have $13.19 in the bank." She said, "That's close enough!"

To God "close enough" is not really close enough. The Great Commandment calls us to love God with every ounce of our being and to love others as we love ourselves. It's the big picture (Mark 12:30-31).

True consecration knows no reservations.

Action Points

✓ Do I understand that Jesus *is* the big picture?
✓ Do I read the Bible understanding who He is?
✓ Have I allowed a picture of Jesus that's not true to His Word?
✓ Do I try to get close enough to get by, or close enough to go deeper?

Think About It

There is a Book worth all other books which were ever printed.
—Patrick Henry

God's delight is received upon surrender,
not awarded upon conquest.
—Max Lucado

*If anyone is in Christ, he is a new creation; the
old has gone, the new has come!*
—2 Cor. 5:17

3

Transformation

God specializes in transforming broken lives.

It was Saturday morning at Taylor County Camp Meeting, near Butler, Georgia. I was 16 years old. Five difficult and painful years had gone by since my father's death. To most observers I was doing quite well. I enjoyed school, excelled academically, and seemed adjusted on the outside. However, I was the only boy in my class without a father at home. That one fact had been my big picture and caused me to feel inferior to my peers.

I tried to compensate with my grades. My straight-A goal possessed me, and I consistently reached it. But it was not enough to fill my empty heart.

As a teenager, the anger and bitterness in my heart toward God increased. I was confused. I wanted to believe that God cared about me, but I couldn't understand why He took my father from me. Increasingly, I blamed God for my pain. My resentment reached the boiling point one July morning as I sat in the rustic old camp meeting tabernacle. I could smell the wonderful aroma of Southern fried chicken as it floated from the camp's dining hall through the hot, humid Georgia air. I prayed for a short service and an early dinner bell. Just then, my fried chicken thoughts took second place as I heard the booming voice of Donald Rollings as he sang,

> Could we with ink the ocean fill,
> And were the skies of parchment made,

Were ev'ry stalk on earth a quill,
And ev'ry man a scribe by trade,
To write the love of God above
Would drain the ocean dry;
Nor could the scroll contain the whole,
Tho' stretched from sky to sky.

—Meir Ben Isaac Nehorai

I realized for the first time how much God loved me. I came to see that God intentionally sent His beloved Son to die on the Cross *for me.* I understood the father-son relationship. Suddenly, the thought that God had given His Son, His dearest treasure for me, overwhelmed me.

I recalled how I stood helplessly and watched my dad die that Christmas Eve morning five years before. I would have done anything to save his life. I recognized that God, the eternal Father, had the power to deliver His Son from the hands of His enemies, that He could have rescued His Son, but He deliberately let him die—for me.

Whenever a person is ready
to uncover his or her sins, God is always
ready to cover them.

I ran to the altar of prayer. I confessed my sins and asked for forgiveness. The old passed away, and I became a new creation in Christ Jesus. With His nail-scarred hands, Jesus picked up the pieces of my shattered dreams and broken heart, and with His mighty power He made my heart whole again. I was transformed!

Hallelujah, what a Savior, Who can take a poor lost
sinner,
Lift him from the miry clay and set him free!
I will ever tell the story, Shouting, "Glory, glory, glory!"
Hallelujah! Jesus ransomed me.

—Julia H. Johnston

The Big Picture Frame

Big picture people
see Jesus as the source of salvation
for everyone, everywhere, who comes
to Him by faith. We cannot be big picture
people unless we experience and
share in transformation.

Erwin Patricio's Transformation

For 16 years my wife, Winnie, and I served with World Gospel Mission as missionaries to the Native Americans in the southwestern United States. That's where we met Erwin Patricio. Erwin grew up in a mud hut on the Tohono O'odham Reservation in southern Arizona. He became an alcoholic in his early teens and went to jail more than 30 times. By age 30 he was known as the reservation drunk.

Erwin felt like a failure. "I've destroyed everything I've touched in life," he confessed.

> No life is so broken that God
> cannot make it whole.

Then Erwin met Jesus.

The transformation was just beginning. Sometime in the growing of his new faith, Erwin heard God's call to preach the gospel.

"Lord, can You make a preacher out of a reservation Indian with less than a sixth grade education?" he asked.

---

*God is forever and forever getting
new mornings out of old nights.*

God was faithful. He worked His miraculous transformation in Erwin's life. Soon he enrolled in Bible college, graduating four years later with academic honors. For more than 20 years Erwin and his beautiful wife, Naomi, have served effectively as missionaries with World Gospel Mission. Hundreds of Native Americans have become followers of Christ because of the faithful witness of the Patricios. The testimony of one of the tribal leaders shares the best confirmation of this transformation: "Erwin is the Billy Graham of our reservation."

---

*Genuine repentance
is a moving condition of the heart
that is testified and demonstrated by our
deeds. It's an inward conviction
that expresses itself in outward actions.*
—Max Lucado

Peter's Transformation

Peter was one of the students Jesus personally selected to attend the "Bible college" He operated for approximately three years. Peter was an outspoken student, but like all the others, he was a slow learner in spite of the fact that the Master Teacher was his only professor.

There were moments when Jesus was pleased with Peter's progress. When Peter stated, "You are the Christ, the Son of the living God," the Teacher praised him for speaking the very thoughts of God (see Matt. 16:15-19). But shortly thereafter, Peter resisted Jesus when the Master tried to explain that His enemies would kill Him. Jesus rebuked Peter sharply, "Get behind me, Satan!" (v. 23).

This exchange in Matt. 16 underscores Peter's spiritual roller coaster. He was clearly self-centered, inconsistent, and confused. Is there any wonder that eventually he denied that he even knew Christ? (26:74).

But Jesus was not finished with Peter. In Acts 2, Peter emptied himself of self-centeredness and self-reliance. Holy love fired his heart. The Spirit of the resurrected Christ filled his heart. Boldness replaced cowardice. Faithfulness overpowered inconsistency. Illumination from the Holy Spirit obliterated confusion.

The highest purpose of faith is
not to change my circumstances,
but to change me.

Dan Smith's Transformation

Dan Smith began sniffing glue at age 12. At age 30 he had a wife and three small children, but he also had a serious addiction to alcohol and drugs. To further complicate matters, he could neither read nor write.

Shortly before his wife died with cancer, she met Jesus in a life-changing way. Through her consistent, loving witness, Dan came to Christ. When his wife died, he was left with the care and responsibility for their three children. He began growing in his new relationship. Soon he heard God's call to preach the gospel. His response was all but calm.

"I have three children to support and care for, and I can't read or write. How can I be a preacher?"

But God provided the answers. Dan earned his general equivalency diploma (GED) in record time. That's when he came to Circleville Bible College in Ohio, where I was president. Quite frankly, it was with reluctance that we enrolled this young man from Pennsylvania. There was every reason to believe he would never succeed at

Bible college—and he wouldn't have without a transformation.

But Dan succeeded and received his bachelor of arts degree in religion. There at college he met and married a talented young woman who worked in the business office. They currently pastor a congregation near Lancaster, Ohio.

Several months ago I preached revival services at their church. During an informal sharing time an elderly lady who had attended the church for many years said, "Pastor Dan is the most loving, caring person I have ever met! I see Jesus when I look at Pastor Dan."

God still transforms a "Saul" to make a "Paul"!

Reach up as far as you can, and God will reach down the rest of the way.

Action Points

✓ Do I see everyone, everywhere, as a candidate for salvation?

✓ Who can I tell my transformation story to?

✓ Where am I involved in another person's transformation?

✓ Am I expending unnecessary energy in areas that do not lead to transformed lives? What can I do about it?

Think About It

A river without banks is only a huge puddle.
—Ken Blanchard

The reason for intercession is
not that God answers prayer,
but that God tells us to pray.
—Oswald Chambers

Let us then approach the throne of grace with
confidence, so that we may receive mercy and
find grace to help us in our time of need.
—Heb. 4:16

4

Prayer Life

God does some things in answer to prayer that
He will not do for any other reason.

We talk about prayer, read about prayer, and attend
seminars about prayer. However, few of us learn to pray
effectively. We spend too much time discussing how to
pray and too little time actually doing it.

Prayer isn't a spiritual function reserved for early
morning or a specific time and place. It's a way of life. It's
constantly acknowledging that I can do nothing without
the Lord's help. It's an unconditional, ongoing surrender
to His will and a moment-by-moment desire for His presence, purity, and power.

The Secret

Two of the most Christlike people I've ever known
were Mr. and Mrs. A. L. Luce Sr. Mr. Luce founded the
Blue Bird Body Company of Fort Valley, Georgia, in 1927.
Blue Bird survived the Great Depression and eventually
became the largest school bus manufacturer in the world.
One day in the dining hall at Indian Springs Camp Meeting in Georgia, I heard a gentleman ask Mr. Luce, "What's
the secret of Blue Bird's success?" He immediately
replied, "My wife's prayers!"

The Big Picture Frame

Big picture people
know that prayer is not a ritual,
but a way of life.

Prayer is the Christian's breath. It's the air we breathe. It's our link with another world. It's our unending cry for the God of heaven to invade our personal space and keep us focused on eternal values and the big picture.

Prayer reminds us that "I am weak, but He is strong." Prayer requires that we must decrease but He must increase (see John 3:30, KJV). Prayer prods us to step aside and permit God to step into every situation with resources only He possesses.

Prayer does not fit us for the better work;
prayer *is* the greater work.
—Oswald Chambers

A Prayer Warrior

At age 18 I married my high school sweetheart, Winnie Orvin. She's a true Southern belle with all the graces, charm, and beauty the term implies. Since May 7, 1960, she's been my loving companion and wonderful ministry partner. While I often serve in the public arena, she has quietly stayed behind the scenes, undergirding me with a life of consistent prayer. Never have I stepped into a spiritual battle without the wonderful assurance that Winnie would be lifting the prayer of faith in my behalf. Recently when our family was facing an unusually difficult and prolonged challenge, one of our children reminded us, "Don't give up! Mom's praying, and great things happen when Mom prays!"

I remember my mother's prayers,
and they have followed me.
They have clung to me all my life.
—Abraham Lincoln

But When We Prayed

When I served as president of Circleville Bible College, I frequently explained to the student body my "open door, open office, open home, open heart" policy. I repeatedly invited the students to share their problems and concerns with me. It was disappointing to observe their hesitancy and fear when they peered into my office. However hesitant, many came and told me about their discouragement. Occasionally a young man or woman would be on the verge of quitting college. But when we prayed, the Holy Spirit brought new strength and determination. Today scores of these young men and women serve Christ around the world as pastors, teachers, and missionaries.

A Bold Entrance

A beautiful young woman arrived on the Circleville campus in the fall of 1986. She never hesitated to visit me and entered my office boldly. She pulled up a chair, placed her elbows on the big desk, and confidently said, "Dad, I need five dollars!"

My daughter, Angie, didn't hesitate to ask for anything. To her I was much more than the president. Our relationship was different. It was a blood relationship, a love relationship. We were family.

Our relationship with the Father is because of the blood of Christ. Royal blood flows in our veins. We are "heirs of God, and joint-heirs with Christ" (Rom. 8:17, KJV). Our Father invites us to come boldly before His throne and find grace to help in times of need (see Heb. 4:16). Prayer is that bold entrance.

Prayer is the opening of a channel
from your emptiness to God's fullness.

Prayer Makes a Difference

God acts in answer to the prayers of His people. Our prayers seem to open the windows of heaven and unlock the provisions of His wonderful grace.

In a Sunday School class one day, a junior high boy asked, "If God wants the whole world to hear the gospel and be saved, why doesn't He announce in a loud voice to the whole earth that Jesus, His Son, is the only Savior, and that He's giving all people one hour to confess their sins and invite Jesus into their hearts?"

Another lad responded, "Perhaps God doesn't speak all languages."

Immediately a young woman chimed in, "Well, He could use interpreters."

The truth is, I don't know why God left to the Church the awesome task and wonderful privilege of taking the name of Jesus to all the world to make disciples of all nations. I simply know that He reaches people through people. Has anyone ever come to Christ without at least one other person somewhere, sometime, being involved in the process? Isn't intercessory prayer always a part of the process?

The highest and greatest calling of
Christians is the ministry of prayer.
—Max Lucado

First Christian Prayers

In a recent review of the Book of Acts, I observed the vital importance of prayer in the lives of the first Christians. The Early Church prayed faithfully, fervently, and frequently. They believed that prayer made a difference! They prayed for courage to faithfully proclaim the name of Jesus, whatever the cost. As William Coker once preached at Camp Sychar in Mount Vernon, Ohio, "The Holy Spirit energized them to proclaim Jesus with their lips, lives, love, liberty, and loot."

The Big Picture Frame

Big picture people believe that prayer links our need to God's abundant supply.

Prayer at 31,000 Feet

On April 14, 1988, I was aboard Piedmont Airlines flight 486 from Charlotte, North Carolina, bound for Columbus, Ohio. When the captain announced at 31,000 feet that he expected a smooth flight to Columbus, I glanced outside and observed the beauty of a warm spring day. There was not a cloud in sight. The West Virginia mountains were carpeted in a gorgeous green that seemed to stretch forever.

Suddenly a loud explosion shattered the peace and tranquillity. It destroyed one engine of our Fokker F28 jet and ripped a huge hole in the aircraft near the galley. We lost cabin pressure instantly. In a few seconds we plunged to 10,000 feet and continued a rapid fall. Now the West Virginia mountains loomed as angry jaws of death ready to swallow us. Fear seized everyone. Death seemed certain.

The captain's voice brought little assurance when he announced that he would attempt an emergency landing in Charleston, West Virginia. His request for prayer was hardly necessary. We were all praying, including many who likely had not prayed for years. One man behind me mixed his pleas to God for mercy with regular outbursts of profanity.

To our amazement, the landing was quite smooth. Looking at all the broken hydraulic lines dangling in the gaping hole, I marveled that the pilot could control the badly damaged aircraft during the delicate landing maneuvers. As soon as the plane touched the ground, several passengers fainted. The pressure of the ordeal was simply more than they could handle.

Several days after this emergency situation, I received a letter from an elderly lady in Alabama. She had regularly prayed for Winnie and me during our years in Arizona, but we had lived in Ohio for eight years. Our contact with this dear lady had been infrequent. She wrote,

> I'm getting old, and my hands shake. I do hope you can read my scribble. I just want you to know that I prayed especially for you on April 14. I was working in my flower garden when God burdened my heart with an overwhelming sense of urgency to pray for your safety.
>
> I hurried to my bedroom and fell on my knees before the Lord. The only words I could utter were these: "O God, Doug Carter is in trouble. Please stretch forth Your mighty hand, place it beneath him, and keep him safe, wherever he may be today." It was at 10:00 in the morning when I was interceding for you.

That was the exact time of the explosion. Would God have preserved my life if she had failed to pray? I can't be certain, but I believe this was one of those moments when God acted in response to the prayers of one of His children.

---

*Every new victory a soul gains
comes as the result of prayer.*
—John Wesley

Action Points

✓ Does my prayer life demonstrate how much I believe prayer matters?

✓ Am I fully convinced that God is able and willing to provide everything I need?

✓ Do I obey the Holy Spirit's faithfulness to prompt me when my prayers could make a difference for someone else?

✓ Is prayer a priority or a postscript to my life?

Think About It

Is prayer a road I regularly travel, or one I use when I can find no easier route?
—Oswald Chambers

You cannot explore the oceans
until you have courage enough
to lose sight of the shore.

Whoever wants to save his life will lose it,
but whoever loses his life for me will save it.
—Luke 9:24

5

Taking Risks

Playing it safe means failure.

$\mathcal{In}$ the parable of the talents, Jesus sharply rebuked the servant who played it safe. He pronounced judgment with these tragic words: "Throw that worthless servant outside, into the darkness" (Matt. 25:30). The servant explained his refusal to become a risk-taker by saying, "I was afraid" (v. 25).

> You can't steal second and
> keep your foot on first.
> —Frederick Wilcox

Taking a Risk

I shared earlier about my confusing teenage years. By age 14, I had become a loner. I was afraid of close relationships. After all, I could lose a friend and experience pain. I came to believe that if I had a close friend, I could be hurt. So I simply avoided such relationships.

One day in high school I discovered Winnie Orvin. Not only was she witty and friendly, but also she was as pretty as an angel. Her smile could melt any heart.

Winnie was a starter on the girls' varsity basketball team. Even though I didn't have enough courage to speak to her, I could attend her games, watch her play, and dream about her. I was there when her team won the state championship, and she shot the winning free throw in a 49-48 thriller. I cheered from the stands, where my fear kept me.

I really wanted to ask her for a date, and I began to pray for the courage to break the stronghold that fear had in my life. Finally, I decided I would ask her younger sister to be my messenger. I reasoned that rejection wouldn't be as painful if relayed through a third person. I almost chickened out before reaching her sister. I came to believe that Winnie Orvin was worth dying for. Even if it killed me, I had to ask her for a date.

I did and lived to tell the rest of the story. Winnie has been my wife for 40 years. We have three wonderful children: Angie, Eric, and Jason, and they have the best mom in the entire world. Some things are worth the risk!

Risk-Takers

Queen Esther was willing to risk everything to deliver her people from genocide. Peter, Paul, Stephen, and many other first-century Christians risked all for the sake of the gospel. Martin Luther and David Livingstone are later examples of risk-takers who made a powerful difference in the history of the Church.

Most of us enjoy the comfort zone. We prefer security to the battlefield. But God has called us to spiritual warfare. We're able to confront the enemy only from the battlefront. It's risky there. The stakes are high. Eternity is the issue.

The Big Picture Frame

Big picture people
know you become a failure
when you fail to take risks.

A Risk-Taker in Africa

Ernie Steury and his wife, Sue, have faithfully served as missionaries in Kenya for almost 40 years. He was the first doctor at Tenwek Hospital—if you can call a one-room building a hospital. He performed surgeries beyond his training, knowing that the death of a patient could cost him his life at the hands of an angry family member.

Today Tenwek is a shining city of hope and healing on the side of a hill. Three hundred beds in modern wards with a well-qualified staff make it one of the largest and best mission hospitals in Africa. Medical intervention has saved thousands of lives.

More important, tens of thousands have found Christ as Savior because of the pioneer leadership of a risk-taker, Dr. Ernie Steury.

The first step to leadership is
servanthood.
—John Maxwell

A Risk-Taker in Honduras

Don and Twana Hawk, Ohio farmers, sold their farm and moved to Honduras, where God had called them. In one of the most dangerous jungle regions of Central America, they carved out a farm and began a school for underprivileged boys. One of their sons almost died when a rabid dog bit him in the jungle. They risked everything to share the name of Jesus in this needy area.

Today El Sembrador, the farm school founded by Don, operates a grade school, high school, vocational school, and Bible institute in modern facilities. Some outstanding Christian leaders in Honduras have come from El Sembrador. David Castro is the national president of the Honduran Holiness Church, a growing denomination of 180 churches. Jorge Pinto serves as vice president as he pastors a congregation of nearly 500. Gumercindo Excovar is a lawyer for the Honduran government.

If God be your partner,
make your plans large.

A Risk-Taker in South America

Meredythe Scheflin has spent her lifetime building schools in Bolivia. Some years ago I visited Bolivia, where Meredythe took me to a large vacant field outside the growing city of Santa Cruz. She said, "God's going to help me build an Evangelical university right here!" I said to myself, "Merry, it's time for you to retire. How can you take on this project at this time in your life?" Even one of Dr. Scheflin's colleagues said to me, "Isn't it a shame that Merry's last project in Bolivia is destined for failure?"

But Meredythe Scheflin didn't believe in failure. She believed that when God gives a dream, He also provides the resources to make the dream become reality. Today the Bolivia Evangelical University enrolls approximately 2,500 students on a beautiful campus in the exact place where Meredythe said it would be.

Most people who succeed in the face of
impossible conditions are people who
simply don't know how to quit.

Merry is now past retirement age, but she's still dreaming. She now believes God will provide a hospital and a television station at the university. She knows the job is too big for her, but stay tuned—God honors risk-takers.

Risk-Takers and Praise

Can you imagine the apostle Paul playing it safe? He was so committed to "the heavenly vision" that in the dungeon at midnight, with his feet in chains and his back bleeding, he could sing hymns of praise and victory (Acts 26:19, KJV; 16:25). I can hear some earlier versions of "Amazing Grace," "Love Lifted Me," "He Brought Me Out," "All Hail the Power of Jesus' Name," "He Touched Me," and "Victory in Jesus." Praise is always on the lips of God's risk-takers.

Action Points

- ✓ Do I play it safe when God wants me to move out of my comfort zone?
- ✓ Do I listen to Satan's doubts about God more than God's truth about Satan?
- ✓ What success waits on my willingness to take a risk for God?
- ✓ How do I respond when difficult circumstances are the result of risks? Do I whine or sing praises?

Think About It

If you want to make a big difference, you must take some risks.

A leader knows the way,
goes the way, and shows the way.
—John Maxwell

*Follow my example, as I
follow the example of Christ.*
—1 Cor. 11:1

6

Leadership

*If you want to be an eagle,
don't spend your time with turkeys.*

Effective leaders know that negative people cast long, dark shadows in an organization. They know that fear of failure or rejection often controls negative people. They know that fear destroys dreams.

On the other hand, effective leaders know that positive people are like sunlight. They bring hope, creativity, optimism, excitement, and energy to a team.

Positive Leaders

I've had the special privilege of working closely with some outstanding, positive Christian leaders. In 1964, when Winnie and I began our missionary service with World Gospel Mission, George R. Warner was president. He was known for his humility and compassion. Later I served with Thomas H. Hermiz, current president, a strong, decisive leader and superb communicator. Today it's my joy to work with John Maxwell of INJOY Ministries. He is a Christian leadership author and speaker whose enthusiasm and humor are powerful communication tools. Another Christian leader whose friendship I value is Stan Toler, known for his incredible people skills and generosity. Then there was my wonderful friend and leadership model, the late George E. Luce, one of three sons of A. L. Luce, founder of the Blue Bird Body Company.

> When the character of a man is not
> clear to you, look at his friends.
> —Japanese proverb

While these men differ in personalities and leader-ship styles, they have at least two things in common. First, they demonstrate a passion for God and His perfect will in their lives. Second, they surround themselves with positive people. They know that attitude is everything.

Team Building

All great leaders are team builders. They're not one-man bands. They know that an individual totally wrapped up in himself or herself is a formula for smallness, not greatness. Instead of trying to do the job alone, they en-list, train, empower, and involve the best people available. They coach and encourage. They share their vision of what God wants to do through the team. They know that dreams motivate positive people.

> A single arrow is easily broken,
> but not 10 in a bundle.
> —Japanese proverb

The best leaders do everything possible to help each member of the team reach his or her potential. They re-joice when team members excel. They recognize and re-ward excellence.

John Maxwell has often said, "Never do ministry alone." In other words, the effective leader is always preparing other leaders by pouring his or her life into them. The great leader has served best when he or she has helped produce other leaders, perhaps even leaders who are more capable and effective than their mentor.

---

*God will give to us what He knows
will flow through us.*

Heroes Help Mold

As a young boy, I often slipped my radio under the covers and listened late at night to broadcasts of the Brooklyn Dodgers. I loved Snider, Reese, Robinson, Hodges, Furillo, Campanella, Erskine, and the other "boys of summer" who played in ancient Ebbetts Field. But I wanted to be like Vin Scully, the Hall of Fame announcer who broadcasted the Dodgers games on radio. His golden voice captivated me.

Then as a teenager I heard Jimmy Lentz preach. What a communicator! His eloquence and delivery mesmerized me. I dreamed of the day when I could preach with the power of Dr. Lentz. In fact, many years later we did preach together on several occasions. From the day I met him until the last camp meeting we preached together, he always encouraged me. He bragged on my preaching and called me "his boy." While I'll never have his skill as a communicator, his words of encouragement often gave me urgently needed reassurance. He gave me more than a model—he poured his life into me. He helped influence the character and direction of my life.

Mentoring Erwin

Erwin Patricio, described earlier, lived in the "pigpen" of life until Jesus radically transformed him. A few years after his conversion, this Native American brother joined the staff at Southwest Indian School as chaplain.

Erwin loved God and cared deeply about the spiritual needs of the students. I soon recognized that he could become an outstanding speaker and Christian leader. I loved his sense of humor and admired his positive outlook on life.

I spent countless hours with Erwin. Each day I looked for ways to encourage him. I sent him notes expressing gratitude for his ministry to students. I talked with him, prayed with him, laughed with him, and cried with him.

Treat a person as he is,
and he will remain as he is.
Treat him as he could be,
and he will become what he should be.
—Anonymous

I tried to convince Erwin that he and Naomi should travel across the United States representing Southwest Indian School in churches and Christian colleges. He quaked at my suggestion. But I continued to assure him that God would use his personal testimony in a powerful way.

At last, the Patricios started on their journey across North America, visiting church after church. Wherever they went, churches experienced an awakening that bordered on and sometimes equaled revival.

As Erwin and Naomi continue to share their steadfast faith and transformed testimony, they have led multitudes to Christ. I rejoice that God allowed me to have a part in their ministry.

The Big Picture Frame

**Big picture people
understand that leadership
is a positive channel to help others
reach their potential in Christ.**

Mentoring sends people where I cannot go. It touches more lives than I can touch. Leadership without mentoring is self-serving.

---

*True leadership must be
for the benefit of the followers,
not the enrichment of the leaders.*

Action Points
✓ Who are the positive leaders who have influenced your life?
✓ Who is your coach at this stage in your leadership development?
✓ Who are you coaching?
✓ Review "Positive Lessons." Which lessons do you need to work on to increase your leadership potential?

Think About It

It's not enough to finish the race yourself. To be successful, you must take somebody with you across the finish line.
—John Maxwell

POSITIVE LESSONS

Through my years in full-time Christian ministry, I have had the opportunity to observe the lives of Christians who possess a positive attitude. Here is what I've learned from them:

1. They refuse to become defensive.
2. They learn from defeats.
3. They look for opportunities to affirm others.
4. They avoid enslavement to things. They know that a collection of possessions on earth does not produce an abundant life. They know that gadgets and toys don't lead to peace and joy.
5. They avoid addiction to busyness. They don't believe that "God will love me more if I do more." Instead, they recognize it as a destructive philosophy.
6. They remember that success is not a destination, but the journey.
7. They take time to have fun. They know that playing can be as spiritual as praying.
8. They value relationships—with God, their families, their friends, and their colleagues.
9. They remember that God has not called us to perfect performance and achievement, but to complete surrender to His Son.
10. They don't expect life to be free of problems. They know that life isn't a quiet stream without waves or storms.
11. They've learned to listen. They value the ideas and opinions of other positive people.
12. They unload guilt. They know that a person is destined for misery until he or she forgets the things that are behind.
13. They remember that they are earthen vessels and subject to mistakes. They don't try to "walk on the water." Instead, they strive for honesty

and transparency as they walk in the power of the Spirit.

14. They believe that one person can make a difference, yet they never forget the vital importance of teamwork.

15. They set high goals that they can reach only with God's help.

To handle yourself, use your head.
To handle others, use your heart.
—John Maxwell

As God's chosen people, holy and dearly loved,
clothe yourselves with compassion, kindness,
humility, gentleness and patience. Bear with
each other and forgive whatever grievances
you may have against one another.
Forgive as the Lord forgave you.
And over all these virtues put on love,
which binds them all together in perfect unity.
—Col. 3:12-14

7

Team Effort

Do unto others as they would have you do unto them.

The effective leader is always you-focused, not me-focused. I call it the "you principle." The leader cares deeply about coworkers and the people to whom they minister. The leader pays attention to the team.

A leader believes in people.
—John Maxwell

Team Building

During my years as director at Southwest Indian School, I worked with a small but very dedicated team of career missionaries. Volunteers made up the majority of the team, usually retired people who were self-supporting. This group of 40 or so came from every part of the United States and at least a dozen denominations. They ranged in age from 23 to 80.

People support what they help create.

It was essential to blend this diverse group into a cohesive team. The Holy Spirit faithfully guided us. The two most experienced missionaries, Noble Wilkinson and Mollie Hensley, covenanted to pray at least one hour each day for me and the others on the leadership team. Prayer fused us together. Praying together as staff early each morning and in our business meetings kept us focused on the vision and united in our efforts.

The Lord can do great things through those who don't care who gets the credit.
—Helen Pearson

Again and again God miraculously provided the financial resources we needed to help fund the vision. For example, one afternoon I received a telephone call from the president of a charitable foundation. While vacationing in our area, they had seen a picture of the senior choir from the Southwest Indian School. As they looked at the faces of the Indian youth, they were strongly impressed to contact the school and ask about the school's financial needs. Within a matter of days, she and her husband sent a donation large enough to pay for the construction of a beautiful new 400-seat chapel-auditorium.

As the team came together, the school experienced steady growth. Enrollment doubled. Many experienced God's transforming work as the team labored for one purpose in many ways. They raised millions of dollars to purchase land, construct 12 buildings, and renovate several older facilities. It was a team effort to equip others to serve the Lord.

The Big Picture Frame

**Big picture people
teach the power of teamwork
and partnership.**

The supreme quality of a leader is
unquestionable integrity.
—Chuck Swindoll

Learning from Three Sons

The 15th chapter of Luke has always been one of my favorite Bible stories. Many don't realize that it tells not about two sons, but three.

1. **The prodigal son** is the one who sought his independence, squandered his inheritance, and almost ate with pigs. Our hearts rejoice when he comes to his senses, admits his sin, and receives his father's unconditional forgiveness. However, his early rebellion shows how independence obscures the way—it does not lead the way.

2. **The proud son.** The older brother is sometimes called "the proud son." At the end of the story, he's the only one who misses the celebration. He seems to have done the right things for the wrong reasons. He was too wrapped up in himself. Wingrove Taylor makes these observations about the elder brother: he exhibited his self-centeredness, he extolled his self-righteousness, he excused his bitterness, and he expected his reward. It's the antithesis to the "you principle." Looking only at himself, he could lead no one.

People who live for themselves are in a
mighty small business.

3. **The perfect son.** Few talk about the third son in Luke 15. He is Jesus, the Son who told the story. He's our beautiful example of servant leadership and team building. He obeyed His Father completely, even though He knew the Cross stood between Him and obedience. He came not to receive ministry, but to minister to others by giving His life for a lost world.

TEAM EFFORT LESSONS

THE PRINCIPLES

Team effort doesn't happen by accident. It takes focused effort from the leader to make it a reality. Here are some lessons in team building that proved important as we set out to reach God's vision for Southwest Indian School.

1. Express the God-given vision for growth and excellence regularly.

2. Clearly communicate and regularly update specific goals.

3. Share consistent information about progress toward the goals.

4. Make every effort to help team members identify and utilize their spiritual gifts.

5. Provide ample opportunities to improve the skills necessary to complete the goals.

6. Keep individual spiritual vitality a priority, and find ways to encourage it.

7. Express gratitude publicly and privately for faithful and effective service.

8. If a team member is not performing adequately, confront the problem with love, and provide an opportunity for additional training or resources to improve performance.

9. Saturate the atmosphere with openness, understanding, and affirmation.

10. Demonstrate to the team your commitment to excellence, personal integrity, and spiritual vitality.

11. Devote top-quality time to building a strong administrative team who will move the whole team toward the vision.

12. Recruit additional positive team members, and make it an ongoing priority.

TEAM EFFORT LESSONS

JESUS' EXAMPLE

Jesus was a team builder. Look at the way He modeled team-building lessons.

1. He showed fishermen a better way to fish. He gave a tax collector a lesson in value. He gave a rebel a new war. Jesus always shared the Kingdom vision.

2. He daily showed His followers how to carry out their only mission: making disciples, baptizing them, and teaching them to obey.

3. He told them when they didn't have enough faith and how they could get more. He told them when His time was near and when it had finally come.

4. He identified leadership in Peter, compassion in John, evangelism in Andrew.

5. He gave on-the-job training for three years.

6. He took the disciples away for private retreat. He shared a mountaintop experience with three leaders. He was always looking for ways to energize their faith.

7. He blessed Peter for his spiritual understanding. He affirmed Mary for choosing better.

8. He rebuked Peter for a misguided focus and later reinstated him as a shepherd.

9. He hid nothing about His motives or His mission. In three years nothing false surfaced.

10. He laid down His life for His team.

11. He taught them the importance of prayer and showed them how to pray. He demonstrated how the team builder serves his team. He even washed their feet.

12. In addition to calling the original 12 disciples, He recruited Mary, Martha, Lazarus, Mary Magdalene, Nicodemus, and others. The recruitment list continues with Paul all the way to you and me.

From the cradle, to the towel and basin, to the Cross, He lived His life for others. In contrast to the prodigal son and his independence and the proud son and his self-centeredness, Jesus forever demonstrated that true servanthood focuses on pleasing the Father while investing lovingly and faithfully in the lives of others.

Leadership is servanthood.
Observance of this truth
keeps your motives pure
and protects you from ambition.
It also makes you like Jesus.
—John Maxwell

The Big Picture Frame

**Big picture people
see possibilities in others and invest time
in helping them reach their potential by
teaching them the power of teamwork.**

The Ultimate Team Sacrifice

Calvary is the ultimate sacrifice. Our Savior's bleeding hands were the hands that fashioned humanity. They were pierced by those He created. The One who created every raindrop pleaded for just one drop of water. In refusing to save himself, He provided salvation for everyone—including those who pounded the nails into His hands.

Kings have always sent
their people out to die for them,
but King Jesus died for His people.
—Ken Blanchard

Action Points

- ✓ Who is your team? Your family? The class you teach? Your staff?
- ✓ How do you protect yourself from a dangerous me-focus in leadership?
- ✓ Review the Team Effort Lessons. Which ones do you need to work on? How will you start?
- ✓ Which son best illustrates your leadership style?
- ✓ Will you allow Jesus to touch a lost world through your heart and hands?

Think About It

When you hire people who are smarter than you are, you prove you are smarter than they are.
—Robert H. Grant

Until God is in control of my life,
I am out of control.
—John Maxwell

*I press toward the mark for the prize of
the high calling of God in Christ Jesus.*
—Phil. 3:14, KJV

8

Bumblebees

God never intended for you to be a bumblebee.

Too many of us flit through life from one project to another, spreading ourselves so thin that we do nothing well. We toy with many activities but give ourselves passionately to nothing. We dabble in everything and concentrate on nothing.

Miscellaneous People

I feel pity for people who have never focused their energy and abilities on a cause that demands their best. They are *miscellaneous* people. They believe in doing a little bit of everything. They try to follow a multitude of voices, decreasing their effectiveness to nearly nothing. Such people carry tons of stress and guilt.

Learn to say no to the good
so you can say yes to the best.

PRIDE Helps

How does a person become a *miscellaneous* person? Simply by accepting too many projects and operating with a "just get by" attitude. Instead, we need to restore PRIDE:

P ersonal
R esponsibility
I n
D elivering
E xcellence

The bumblebee lifestyle is a sure pathway to ineffective leadership and exhaustion. The effective leader establishes priorities, knowing that one person can't do everything. Sometimes our commitment to Christ demands that we do less, not more. We need to drop some good activities in order to passionately embrace a cause that makes a difference.

I do only one thing at a time,
and I do it with all my might.
—John Wesley

A Slow Learner

I was a slow learner in this area of my life. Quite early in my ministry at Circleville Bible College, I began to pile one activity onto another onto another onto another. In addition to my duties as president, I maintained a heavy travel and speaking schedule, presided over the local Chamber of Commerce, chaired the visitors' bureau and economic growth council in our community, umpired Little League baseball games, and served on numerous denominational boards and committees—to name just a *few* activities. I was in over my head, and I was tired! I was beginning to neglect my wife, my children, my health, and my relationship with the Lord.

I had become a bumblebee.

The surest way to mishandle a problem
is to avoid facing it.

Realizing one day that my calendar was controlling me, I decided that it was time for *me* to control my calendar. I prayerfully sought guidance from the Holy Spirit, and He helped me establish a list of priorities. Once my

The Big Picture Frame

Big picture people

refuse to be overexposed

and underdeveloped.

priorities were clear, I began the process of reordering my life. Here are the priorities that remain important to me.

1. MY RELATIONSHIP WITH GOD

I am obsessed with knowing Christ. I want the fire of holy love to burn brightly in my heart. I want to experience the infilling of the Holy Spirit daily. Making this a priority means that I reserve time to be alone with God. I'm determined to experience His joy in full measure and spend my life celebrating His grace.

If you want to bring under control a fast-paced lifestyle, you must eliminate the unnecessary; if you want to be where God wants you to be, you must concentrate on the necessary.
—Max Lucado

The world wants your best, but God wants your all.

2. MY WIFE AND CHILDREN

Winnie and I "date" on a regular basis. We reserve dates on the calendar for the two of us to get away for a few hours or even a few days. A loving getaway with one's spouse is more important than teaching a dozen seminars on marriage enrichment. In addition to scheduling time with my wife, I reserve time for my children. I learned that my children didn't need me to give them more things; rather, they needed me to give them an occasional afternoon.

A successful marriage requires falling in love many times, always with the same person.
—Mignon McLaughlin

---

3. MY HEALTH

I try to follow a low-fat, low-carbohydrate diet and walk almost every day. Can we honestly call Jesus our Lord if we don't apply His Lordship to our physical bodies? I have observed that many Christian workers abuse their health. You've probably heard about the overweight pastor who got down to do pushups and discovered he was already up! He's the same gentleman who lamented, "I dieted once for two weeks, and all I lost was 14 days."

You are no more at liberty to throw away your health than to throw away your life.
—John Wesley

> More people commit suicide with
> a fork than with a gun.

There is an unmistakable link between health and effective leadership. Anything that affects your health affects your leadership. Placing the importance of health before ministry makes sure we don't allow ministry demands to crowd out time to take care of ourselves physically.

4. MY MINISTRY

I'm committed to excellence in Christian service. I realize that effective ministry is never a solo performance. It's always a duet with the Holy Spirit. I read at least one book for every week of the year. In my view, there's little difference between the person who can't read and the one who won't read.

> The moment you stop learning,
> you stop leading.
> —John Maxwell

Protect yourself from becoming a *miscellaneous* person. Stop acting like a bumblebee. Control your calendar. Eliminate some activities. Reject mediocrity, and reach for the best in all you do.

> Sometimes it takes hard decisions to bring
> our life under control and realign our
> priorities, focusing on the Father and
> letting everything else take a backseat.

Remember: some things can be left undone. Some things don't matter. A hound dog can whip a skunk, but it isn't really worth it!

Don't Settle for a Triple

Our boys, Jason and Eric, loved Little League baseball. Jason was always small for his age, yet he was consistently one of his team's best hitters. Responding to size without knowing his history, opposing coaches always moved the outfielders in close when Jason stepped to the plate for the first time.

One afternoon Jason pounded the ball over the left fielder's head. His tiny legs raced around the bases and headed for home plate. Jason and the ball reached home plate at about the same moment. The umpire yelled, "Out!"

Jason lay motionless on home plate. Thinking he was injured, I ran toward the field. When I arrived, I heard him sobbing. The tears formed streaks down his dirty face. "Son, why are you crying?"

He answered between sobs, "Because I made an out!"

I began to brag on his great hit. I assured him that it was a tremendous accomplishment to hit a triple. He retorted, "Who wants to settle for a stupid triple when he could have a home run?"

Perhaps you and I don't consider ourselves heavy sluggers, but we do need a burning commitment to reach for the highest. We need to give ourselves passionately to an all-consuming cause. We need to reach our goals. As John Maxwell says, "They don't tally home runs at third base."

Whatever you do, do it with all your might.
Work at it, early and late,
in season and out of season,
not leaving a stone unturned,
and never deferring for a single hour
that which can be done just as well now.
—P. T. Barnum

Make Excellence a Way of Life

Our son Eric has always pursued excellence. He graduated from high school with a perfect 4.0 grade point average. When he entered college, we didn't pressure him to match his high school record. He did it anyway. He completed a bachelor's degree in three years while maintaining a perfect 4.0 grade point average and received early acceptance into the Indiana University School of Medicine.

Eric's high school football coach commented on Eric's phenomenal academic accomplishments in college. He said, "I'm not at all surprised. Excellence is a way of life for Eric."

Perhaps you and I are not 4.0 scholars, but an unwavering commitment to excellence can be our way of life. We can reach for the highest in all we do.

Excellence with Christ

Nowhere is excellence more critical to the Christian leader than with his or her relationship with Christ. Countless Christians play around in the wading pool of spiritual experience, settling for a minimum relationship with Christ. We need to dive into the deep end of the pool, explore the vast reservoir of His grace, and experience Christ to the maximum. We can dabble in everything and leave a blur, or we can focus on God's priorities and make a difference.

No one ever said on his or her deathbed,
"I wish I'd spent more time at the office."

Tuning the Engine

From time to time we need to fine-tune our lives in the same way we give our automobiles regular tune-ups. We must make sure that our spiritual "engines" don't operate at less than maximum power.

My mother-in-law is a quiet, graceful, Southern lady. In her mid-80s, she still lives alone, does her own housekeeping, and drives her car. One day she observed that the car's motor was running somewhat erratically. When she told one of her grandsons about it, he replied, "Grandma, you drive too slowly. You need to put the pedal to the metal and blow out the carbon!"

At the earliest opportunity she followed her grandson's advice. Depressing the accelerator with all her strength, the car soon exceeded the speed limit by at least 30 miles per hour—a regular Jeff Gordon.

Then it happened. There was no mistaking the blue lights flashing in the rearview mirror. When the state trooper walked up to her door, he was amazed to discover that the speeding driver was a small, gray-haired lady. He smiled but restrained his laughter as she explained that she was following her grandson's counsel to correct the engine's problem by driving at full speed.

A quick glance at her driver's license confirmed her age. Since the officer believed there was nothing but honesty on her face, he returned her license, patted her shoulder, and said, "Please slow down." The last thing she saw as she drove away was the policeman doubled over in laughter.

Grandma Orvin used the wrong counsel to solve her engine difficulties. She needed a qualified mechanic who had the expertise and resources to make the necessary adjustments.

As Christians who need regular spiritual renewal, we need triple-A help from our **A**bsolutely **A**dequate **A**dvocate (see 1 John 2:1-6, KJV). He stands ready, willing, and able to help us make engine adjustments and keep up from unnecessary bumblebee behavior.

Action Points

✓ Am I behaving like a bumblebee because I have over-scheduled and overcommitted?

✓ Am I a *miscellaneous person* in the way that I do enough to get by?

✓ Take time to compare the four priorities from this chapter with last week's calendar. What needs to change this week? Schedule it.

✓ Which one of the priorities do I need an accountability partner to make sure I address responsible changes? Who will that partner be?

✓ How do I make excellence my goal in my relationship with Christ?

✓ Where do I need a tune-up?

Think About It

To go nowhere,
follow the crowd.
—John Maxwell

God loves us so much
that sometimes
He gives us what we need
and not what we ask.
—Max Lucado

The God of all grace,
who called you to his eternal glory in Christ,
after you have suffered a little while,
will himself restore you and
make you strong, firm and steadfast.
—1 Pet. 5:10

9

Difficult Times

The sweetest grapes always follow the most bitter winters.

When we moved from Arizona to Ohio, our daughter, Angie, entered junior high school. She tried out for the cheerleading squad and just missed the cut. It broke her heart. As I drove her home from school, she wept bitter tears. I tried to find words with which to encourage her, but nothing seemed to console her. Several days later I apologized to her for my inability to encourage her when she was so heartbroken. She replied, "Dad, I couldn't see you through my tears, but just knowing you were there was all the encouragement and comfort I needed."

The Big Picture Frame

Big picture people
know God is at work even when difficult
times make it hard to see Him.

No matter the difficulty, we must remember that our Father is always there. That's the big picture. He has not promised that a Christian's life will be easy. Nothing in Scripture suggests that God's people will live in a perpetual bubble bath of good feelings and good fortune. Quite to the contrary, we're engaged in real spiritual warfare.

Difficult Times Develop Us

I heard Dennis Kinlaw say to a group of ministers, "God loves us too much to let life be too easy." In other words, if life is too easy, we'll likely become lazy and complacent. Our faith grows when it's tested. It's in the storm that we learn to trust Him completely. It's in the difficult times that we become firmly anchored to Him, who is the bedrock of our faith.

From infancy our daughter, Angie, suffered with asthma. I'll never forget the long night vigils with her as she struggled for her next breath. She took the strongest medication possible, and we followed all the doctor's instructions. Still, nothing seemed to help. I knelt down in the middle of one very long night. As I did, I felt as though God had stepped into the room. He put His loving arms around me and whispered, "Trust Me." I replied, "Lord, I trust You. Please help me to trust more!" No sooner was the prayer out of my heart than I realized that the fear and anxiety were gone as well—and Angie began to breathe normally.

There were other long nights as well, but slowly I learned that if I anchored my faith in Jesus, there was no reason to fear.

Faith Examples

- The story of Joseph is one about faith in the fiery crucible of life. In the middle of rejection, false accusations, prison isolation, his faith survived stronger than ever.

- The Book of Job is about faith—a faith matured through

suffering. It teaches that God has not guaranteed us a life of ease.

- Paul's faith was constantly on trial. His faithful endurance produced the most influential Christian leader of his day.

- Abraham learned that faith requires waiting on the Lord. Even when he struggled with God's timetable, he waited and learned that God always keeps His promises.

God desires to prepare a faithful people whom He can trust in the most difficult places on the battlefield. He's looking for those who will remain faithful when the battle rages. Where are those who will serve Him in the dark, desperate, lonely places? Faith doesn't command God to do our will; rather, it unconditionally accepts His will.

Faith is a deliberate confidence in the character of God, whose ways you may not understand at the time.
—Oswald Chambers

Rev. M. J. Wood

My pastor during my boyhood days was a man who lived a faith example right before my eyes. He obeyed God's call to Christian ministry, even though it meant leaving a key position with a large manufacturing firm where he was headed for financial success.

When he arrived in my hometown to pastor our struggling congregation, he had already planted other churches and established two growing camp meetings. We soon learned that his faith was as large as God's promises. Even when the church couldn't pay him very much, he trusted God to provide. There was always food and clothing for seven children. He even sent his children to excellent Christian colleges!

His faith test came when he led a crusade to legally

eliminate the sale of alcoholic beverages in our county. Many friends advised him to give up the fight. Death threats placed the lives of his entire family at risk. He simply prayed for his enemies, witnessed to them about God's love and grace, and walked away without harm.

Circumstances do not make you what you are — they reveal what you are.
—John Maxwell

As a teenager, I watched this man's faith in action. He became my hero as well as my spiritual mentor. I am only one of many men and women who are in Christian ministry today because of his faith example.

Bitter Winter Sweetness

I was traveling with a tour group by motor coach southward through the Jordan River Valley in Israel. Observing the beauty of the grapevines in the area, I said to our Jewish guide, "Those are the most beautiful vines I've ever seen."

He responded, "Yes, the vines look great, but the grapes won't be very sweet this spring." Noticing my puzzled look, he added, "It's because the winter has been too mild." After a pause he explained, "The sweetest grapes always follow the most bitter winters."

The Big Picture Frame

Big picture people
understand that difficult times produce
faithful workers for the harvest.

Storms

I think most of us understand the importance of rain. During our 16 years of living in the Arizona desert, we frequently heard people say, "Where water flows, Arizona grows." It was true. In places where water was available, things grew. But the absence of water meant desolation and death. And beyond Arizona, from the azaleas and magnolias of the Deep South to the rose gardens and tall timber of the Pacific Northwest, there is abundant evidence that adequate rainfall sustains life and creates beauty.

Yes, we can appreciate the rain. But storms are another matter! I remember the violent thunderstorms that frequented southern Georgia and the terrible dust storms in Arizona that could turn noonday brilliance into midnight darkness. I've seen the tragic aftermath of hurricanes, tornadoes, earthquakes, and flooding.

I like them even less when they move through my life, even though spiritual victories often come in the midst of storms. A storm brought the prophet Jonah to a place of genuine repentance (2:1-9). A storm helped the disciples recognize who Jesus was (Mark 4:41).

Storm Calming

One day Jesus invited His disciples to journey with Him by boat across the Sea of Galilee. He said, "Let us go over to the other side" (Mark 4:35). He did not say, "Let us go halfway across the lake and drown." The disciples must not have heard Him clearly. When the sudden storm descended, they were afraid and even a little angry that He could sleep soundly while they trembled in their sandals. They woke Him with a rebuke. Instead of responding to them, Jesus spoke to the storm. The sea became perfectly calm. The disciples marveled at such power and authority. I can almost hear Him say to them, "Didn't I say we were going to the other side? Did I mention anything about going halfway and drowning? Don't you know that when I am on board, you can travel safely through any storm?"

It's true that Jesus can calm a storm. On the other hand, there are times when He allows the storm to continue and calms our hearts instead. Experiencing peace in the middle of a storm is indescribably wonderful.

Am I close enough to God to feel secure
even when He is silent?
—Oswald Chambers

While none of us ask God to unleash winter's cold blast or a storm's fury upon us, we do need to remember that difficult times can make us more Christlike if we learn to trust Him totally. Bitter or better? We decide.

I have set my sails.
All winds that blow shall
drive me forward.
—Mrs. Charles E. Cowman

The Most Destructive Storm

The storm that concerns me the most is the storm that destroys the harvest. I spent countless summer days during my boyhood picking cotton. Believe me—you've never worked hard until you've picked cotton all day under the burning sun and high humidity of southern Georgia. I recall one summer when the cotton was ready for harvest. Beautiful snowy white fields stretched mile after mile. Late one afternoon, the clouds began to gather in the eastern sky. Soon the clouds darkened, and lightning thundered across the horizon. The wind, rain, and hail pounded the cotton crop into the ground. Bales and bales of cotton were lost. As a result, farmers were unable to adequately feed and clothe their families that season. Some farmers even lost their farms to bankruptcy.

Jesus said to His disciples, "Open your eyes and look at the fields! They are ripe for harvest" (John 4:35). Jesus also said to His followers, "Go into all the world and preach the good news to all creation" (Mark 16:15). The Great Commission is still our big picture.

Be zealous! Be active! Time is short!
—John Wesley

Return to the Big Picture

Bitter winters help develop people who can see the big picture. They help develop people who can fulfill His command to go into all the world and make disciples. But we don't go alone or without protection.

- **We go under His supreme power.**
  All authority in heaven and on earth has been given to me (Matt. 28:18).

- **We go to fulfill His supreme purpose.**
  Go and make disciples of all nations, baptizing them in the name of the Father and of the Son and of the Holy Spirit, and teaching them to obey everything I have commanded you (Matt. 28:19-20).

- **We go surrounded with His supreme presence.**
  Surely I am with you always, to the very end of the age (Matt. 28:20).

A Big Picture Opportunity

While serving as director of a mission school in Arizona for Native American children, a group of dedicated Christian men and women came from Oregon for several weeks of volunteer work on a new school building. One of the men, a banker, was working in a very deep ditch installing a sewer pipe. I noticed two Navajo boys lying face-down on the ground and peering down at the man in the ditch. As I walked up behind the boys, I heard one of them ask the man, "Are you getting paid to do this?" When he answered, "No," one of the boys countered, "Then why are you doing such hard, dirty work down in that ditch?" That's when the man explained that he was there because of his love for Jesus and boys like them.

Two weeks after the man returned to his Pacific Northwest home, he mailed me a written report of his visit. The title captivated me: "How to Have a Mountaintop Experience While Working in the Bottom of a Sewer Ditch." This big picture person did not complain about hot, sweaty work in a ditch. Instead, he rejoiced over the privilege to share his faith with two boys who needed to know Jesus.

This is a time of unprecedented opportunity for world evangelization. Doors have opened to areas long closed to the preaching of the gospel. If you listen, you can hear the Macedonian calls in record numbers from every part of our globe. There is an urgent need for God-called missionaries. When we develop effective, Christlike leaders, multiplication, not addition, results. That's the passion behind EQUIP—Encouraging Qualities Undeveloped In People. In 1996 John Maxwell established this organization to focus on practical leadership development. The persons involved in this ministry are passionately committed to reaching the world for Christ. But this can't happen without strong spiritual leaders in every nation of the world. (For more information, see the appendix.)

We need leaders who will plant churches, equip people for ministry, and reach communities for Christ. We need Great Commission Christians to lift them in prayer and to support them financially. We need them now—before more storms come, while the harvest is ready.

Action Points

✓ Am I tempted to forget the big picture in the face of difficulties?

✓ Am I close enough to God to feel secure even during a storm?

✓ Am I concerned more about the storms that threaten my picture or that threaten God's picture?

✓ Do I understand that the supreme power and presence of Jesus Christ are to help me accomplish His supreme purpose?

✓ Do I see a ripe harvest? What am I doing about it for Jesus' sake?

Think About It

God chooses what we go through; we choose how we go through it.

—John Maxwell

Giving is not God's way
of raising money;
it's God's way
of raising people
into the likeness of His Son.

*Not that I am looking for a gift,
but I am looking for what may be credited
to your account.*
—Phil. 4:17

10

The Personal Factor

Increase your influence by linking your life with others.

When my family and I moved to Indiana in 1989, we located in Gas City, a community of about 6,000 people. I soon learned that one political party had dominated the city's government for almost three decades. As a Christian and a conservative, I often encourage God's people to become involved in the political process. I never dreamed that after two years as a resident of Gas City, God would lead *me* to run for a seat on the city council.

Because of other time-consuming responsibilities, I decided that my campaign would consist of newspaper ads and a letter or two to my constituents. One afternoon I shared my campaign strategy with an elderly gentleman in my neighborhood. He said, "Doug, your situation is hopeless unless you knock on every door in this ward and personally ask people to vote for you!"

I took his advice. For the next two months I spent countless evenings in the living rooms of people in my ward. I listened to them. I shared my vision with them. I formed very special friendships with them. I looked them in the eye and personally asked for their prayers and their support.

Another candidate, my close friend Jim Spurgeon, followed a similar strategy. Both of us were elected. One veteran political observer described our victory as the greatest upset in the history of Gas City. A longtime resident said, "Carter and Spurgeon restored two-party government to our community." One reporter called our win a miracle. It happened because we cared enough about the cause to personally ask others for their support and involvement.

If you would win a man to your cause,
first convince him
that you are his sincere friend.
—Abraham Lincoln

Three Keys

One of my major responsibilities at World Gospel Mission was to teach the biblical method for raising financial support for ministry. Since World Gospel Mission is an interdenominational missions organization, its missionaries must raise their own salaries. We invested hours in discussing the importance of direct appeals by mail and church presentations. However, I always insisted that there are three key ways to raising support effectively:

1. Ask people personally.
2. Ask people personally.
3. Ask people personally.

Most of us are reluctant to ask people *personally* to join our team, especially when it involves a financial commitment. We're more comfortable asking a large group. In a large group, we don't treat a refusal as *personal* rejection. However, focusing on one individual hurls the possibility of rejection into the danger zone.

Just Ask

Although Charles Lindbergh became famous when he

flew across the Atlantic Ocean alone, I've discovered that very little is accomplished in life without the help of others. I learned the importance of asking others to help me reach my God-given goals in a time of tremendous need and great opportunity.

The leaders of World Gospel Mission gave permission for Southwest Indian School to develop a modern campus provided we raised the majority of the needed funds in Arizona and neighboring states. I realized that the future of this ministry was at stake.

I'll never forget one of my first visits in the home of a very wealthy gentleman. When he asked what the school needed, I panicked. We needed $80,000, but I asked for $500. He gave $500.

A few days later this dear gentleman telephoned me. He said, "Because you are young and need to learn an important lesson, I'm going to give you a second opportunity to tell the truth about your need." After a few seconds of silence he added, "What do you need?"

I whispered, "Eighty thousand dollars for a building."

He replied, "Speak up!"

I repeated with more volume, "Eighty thousand dollars."

He chuckled and said, "I thought you would never ask. I'll take care of the building. You'll receive a check soon."

I don't think I need to explain how much I learned that day about the priority of asking and asking honestly.

Leadership functions only
on the basis of truth.
—John Maxwell

No Substitute

An excerpt from a note of a missionary couple who attended one of our support development seminars at

World Gospel Mission shares how they learned the importance of asking people personally to invest in God's work. The wife wrote, "We came home from Support Development Institute and began immediately to utilize everything we had learned about personally asking God's people for support. . . . I am happy to report that the Lord has blessed our efforts, and, in only four months and one week of deputation, we are 96 percent funded! Praise the Lord for His gracious provision!"

It's Not About Money

People sometimes call me a fund-raiser. Many who use the term don't intend it as a compliment. A friend tried to comfort me with the following statement from D. L. Moody: "Blessed are the fund-raisers, for in heaven they shall live next door to the martyrs."

Quite honestly, my goal has never been to raise funds. It's been to help raise people to a greater likeness to Christ. Christ is the ultimate giver. We are most like Christ when we give generously, lovingly, and selflessly.

The giver is always more important than the gift. My priority focuses on spiritual ministry to the giver. My goal is to build lasting friendships with faithful ministry partners and to provide them with opportunities to lay up treasures in heaven.

The Big Picture Frame

Big picture people
don't raise money;
they raise people
to reflect the giving nature of Christ.

Back to Basics

How desperately we need to learn the basics of Christian stewardship! God owns everything; we own nothing. He places in our hands certain resources (time, talent, and treasures) that we are to use for His honor and glory in the building of His kingdom. What a privilege! What a responsibility!

---

*I have held many things in my hands
and lost them all;
but the things I have placed in God's
hands—those I always possess.*
—Earline Steelburg

The Personal Factor

No leadership will be effective without the personal factor. Jesus was a master of this. The Bible gives us more examples of Jesus' *personal* interchanges with people than those of His mass communication events. Mass evangelism produces converts, but the only way to disciple new believers is to become personally involved with them. The Great Commission commands that we go where we can make personal contact with people who need the Good News. Even when going into all the world requires financing family moves, funding medical and educational facilities, and building places of worship, the "going" always includes personally involving people in spreading the Good News. Never hesitate to give people a personal invitation to invest in an eternal opportunity, even when it involves money.

---

*We exist temporarily through
what we take, but we live forever
through what we give.*
—Douglas M. Lawson

Action Points

- ✓ Do I ask personally when I have a vacancy to fill, a project to staff, or money to raise?
- ✓ Do I communicate the whole need or just the part I think someone might agree to?
- ✓ Does my leadership model demonstrate how I want to reflect the giving nature of Christ?
- ✓ Where am I raising people to share in the joy of giving?

Think About It

When God blesses you,
He always has more
than you in mind.
—Ron Jutze

There is always the afterward
of His precious promising.
—Kenneth MacKenzie

*Wait for the LORD; be strong and take heart
and wait for the LORD.*
—Ps. 27:14

11

Waiting

God's afterwards are worth the wait.

The 17th chapter of Matthew begins with these words: "After six days . . ." For those of us who are action people, six days can be a painfully long wait. I know I have many faults, but procrastination isn't one of them. If something needs to be done, I want to do it, and I want to do it *now*. Waiting isn't easy for me. I hate delays. However, I've slowly learned that God's time line may be very different from mine. I think I learned that from my mother first.

From very early in my mother's Christian life, she dreamed about serving as a missionary. However, her dream seemed impossible as her life took unexpected turns. She realized that no one would send a widow with two children to be a missionary in another country. So she lovingly ministered to her children and joyfully served in her local church and community. Her Christlike servanthood impacted the lives of all who knew her.

At the age of 65 she received an invitation to visit a mission field. Her visit turned into 7 years of effective, fruitful service as she led many Native American youth to Christ. Mom often referred to her retirement years, as a missionary, as the most wonderful days of her life.

God is never late, even though sometimes He seems to wait until the last minute!

Waiting with a Promise

Abraham is an Old Testament patriarch we remember for great faith. He discovered that waiting is the ultimate test of faith. God promised Abraham a son, so he waited—and waited, and waited for his son of promise to be born. Finally his faith staggered, and he decided to take matters into his own hands. Even to this day we can track the terrible violence and hatred between Arabs and Jews in the Middle East to Abraham's failure to wait for God to act.

God's time is always the best time.
—John Wesley

Yes and No

Sometimes God, in wisdom and love, says no to our requests. If we wait for the Lord, we'll see the wisdom of His no. What a tragedy it would be if God granted all our foolish petitions!

I have lived to thank God that not all of my prayers have been answered.
—Anonymous

On the other hand, there are many times that God says yes to a plea. We find that the answer is on the way almost before we utter the prayer.

But more and more I have learned that our Father says, "Yes, but not now." Then He instructs us to wait. He declares, "Trust Me, and I will provide at the right time and in the right way that will bless and benefit you the most."

Never think that God's delays are God's denials.

Getting Ready for Yes

When one of my boys was quite small, he asked me for a shotgun. I knew that he loved the outdoors, and he gave every evidence that he would become an avid hunter. However, I felt that he was too young to responsibly handle a firearm. My answer to his request was "Yes, but not now." He wasn't ready for the gift, even though he didn't agree with my assessment. He had some more growing up to do before he was ready for the big responsibility that was required.

Several years later I gave him his first shotgun. It wasn't as large and powerful as he desired, but he was grateful. He handled the gun safely and wisely and proved that he could be trusted with a more powerful weapon. He still loves the outdoors, and hunting remains one of his favorite recreational activities.

The Big Picture Frame

Big picture people
understand that God
uses waiting to prepare His people
for the right answers to their prayers.

Waiting Makes Us Ready

When God says, "Wait," He isn't trying to make us miserable. He doesn't delay because He is temporarily out of supplies and needs to replenish His storehouse. The wait isn't for His benefit; it's for ours. Waiting provides an opportunity for discipline, faith, trust, and obedience to grow in us. Disciplined, obedient waiting matures our faith and lays the foundation for a relationship with the Father that seeks intimacy *with* Him more than gifts *from* Him.

Our Wait

Angie, our firstborn, arrived in our ninth year of marriage. The waiting had at times been agonizingly painful and confusing. We had believed that God would give us a child, but we couldn't understand the delay. Nevertheless, we were determined to do His will. Child or no child, we would obey His call upon our lives and faithfully serve Him.

When I looked into Angie's tiny face only moments after her birth, the long wait was quickly forgotten. I can assure you that God's gift was worth the wait. Let me state with appropriate humility that this miracle baby grew up to become an attractive, intelligent, multitalented young woman. Of course, she got her good looks from her dad— because her mother still has hers!

Angie's Wait

After earning two college degrees and teaching for several years, Angie was more than ready for "Mr. Right" to enter her life. But every would-be prince who came along proved to be a toad. Sad and discouraged, she almost concluded that God didn't care about her and her future. One evening she whispered to God, "I desire You more than anything else in life. My life is totally Yours, single or married, and I want only Your perfect will and plan." Less than a week later, God sent the man of her dreams. Todd and Angie knew almost immediately that God had perfectly prepared them for each other. Today they enjoy great joy and happiness because they were willing to wait.

Faith has nothing to do with
circumstances;
it deals entirely with the Word of God.
—Mrs. Charles E. Cowman

Almond or Mulberry?

I like what Charles Spurgeon says about waiting for the Lord, that some of God's promises are like almond trees, whose blossoms come in early spring. Others are like a mulberry tree, which produces leaves late. It is not easy to know whether you have an almond tree promise or a mulberry tree promise. When answers don't come, the problem is not with the promise. The problem is that we don't wait long enough. Since God has all the time in the world, waiting doesn't rob us of anything—only our failure to wait will.

When you don't know what to do—wait.

Action Points

- ✓ Do I tend to take matters into my own hands rather than wait for God's timing?
- ✓ Do I thank God for His no as well as His yes?
- ✓ Do I trust God enough to wait, even when the waiting is painful or confusing?
- ✓ Do I recognize that waiting prepares *me* for God's answer and *God's answer* for me?
- ✓ Do I know what I'm waiting for—my will or God's?

Think About It

Faith is like a kite:
a contrary wind
causes it to rise.

What is this holiness that God expects of His people? It is a life totally dedicated to Him in obedience.
—Keith Drury

Jesus said to his disciples, "If anyone would come after me, he must deny himself and take up his cross and follow me."
—Matt. 16:24

12

⚞

Commitment

The way up is down.

In John 12, Jesus attempts to explain to His followers the reason for His mission to earth. I see Him hold a small seed in His hand as He says, "Unless a kernel of wheat falls to the ground and dies, it remains only a single seed" (v. 24). He knew that He was born to die. He knew that the Cross stood in the center of the path of obedience to His Father's will.

If Jesus had bypassed Calvary, you and I would be hopelessly lost. There would be no "fountain filled with blood / Drawn from Immanuel's veins" (William Cowper). There would be no grace, no mercy seat. We would be forever under the sentence of eternal death.

But Jesus walked the road of obedience. Like a seed, He died. Now He reproduces His life in you and me. We're the fruit of His obedience, His surrender, His death, and His resurrection.

Peter

In chapter 3 we looked at the transformation that occurred in Peter's life when he allowed the Spirit of the resurrected Christ to live through him. This changed the nature and quality of his commitment. After Pentecost, Peter affirmed with his life, not just his words, that Jesus is the Christ, the Son of the living God. There was no place in his commitment for the self-seeking attitudes that created such inconsistencies at first.

Love is what's left in a relationship after all the selfishness has been removed.

When Peter gave himself fully to the unrestrained work of the Spirit of Christ, it produced a new and deeper commitment, not possible with promises or even the most admirable of human characteristics.

God sends no one away except those who are full of themselves.
—Dwight L. Moody

His Rerun

If we would be disciples of Christ, we must lose our lives and find them in Christ. We must be so totally under His control that our lives become reruns of His life. When we crown Jesus as Lord of all in our hearts, there's no place for self-centeredness to share the throne. Giving Christ complete control also gives Him complete freedom to live through us, love through us, and minister through us. His life reshapes everything—our actions, reactions, attitudes, values, choices, and priorities—so that people see His beauty in everything that makes up our lives.

Christ will have no servants except by consent. His people are a willing people. He will be all in all, or He will be nothing.
—John Wesley

God can't fill our hearts until He empties our hands. We have to release our grip on our lives and give control to Christ. When He takes over, He does so by flooding us with His peace, power, and purity. Christ cannot live His life through us any other way.

Paul said it best: "I have been crucified with Christ and I no longer live, but Christ lives in me. The life I live in the body, I live by faith in the Son of God, who loved me and gave himself for me" (Gal. 2:20).

Yes!

We lay ourselves down. He picks us up. We fall like seeds into the ground to emerge with new life that bears little resemblance to a dead seed. We give up all rights to enjoy all riches in Christ. It's an excruciating exchange. There's only one word that initiates the exchange: *yes.*

Think about a commanding general who issues an order. Can you imagine a private responding, "Sir, I'll have to think about it"? Of course not. A good soldier always obeys his commanding officer.

Jesus is either in full control, or He is not. If you are a fully committed follower of Jesus, your response to your Commander in Chief is always the same: YES.

The essential part of Christian holiness
lies in giving your heart wholly to God.
—John Wesley

What Happened to Commitment?

Commitment is the key. However, commitment is a rare commodity in America today. People break promises too easily. They forget vows. They ignore contracts. I remember when a person would rather die than break a promise, when a person's word was his or her bond, when a handshake was as binding as a written contract. I remember when professional athletes were committed to their team and the game instead of the highest bidder, when there were no holdouts when the season began, when players *and* owners honored their contracts. I especially remember when people considered wedding vows as permanent; when marriage was based on total, absolute, and permanent commitment; and husbands and wives lived out their commitment to each other.

What happened to commitment? Does anyone remember what it really is?

Important Components

Commitment consists of vision, decision, union, and discipline. To shortchange any one of the components is to end up with something other than commitment. Nor can you pick only one of the factors. Commitment is all or nothing. Let me show you what I mean as it applies to my marriage commitment.

The Vision. When Winnie and I were dating, we began to dream about a Christian home with children who loved the Lord. We dreamed of serving together in the Lord's work. While the vision wasn't the reality, it prepared us to take the next step.

The Decision. Our dream moved us to a decision. We willfully, intentionally, and permanently decided to give ourselves to each other. It was a decision that continued to shape other decisions. For example, we set a wedding date, but the date wasn't the commitment. It was simply another step in forging it.

The Union. Finally, our decision brought us to that exciting day when we exchanged vows. I vowed my life to her, and she vowed hers to me. In the overlap of our vows, our lives were in position to become one. Everything that followed would either add to or subtract from the union.

The Discipline. We soon discovered that the quality of our relationship depended on our daily choices. The wedding ceremony was only the starting point. We had to renew our vows every day. Even when the pressures of career, children, and finances tried to rob us of time with each other, we stubbornly determined that our relationship with God and each other would be our highest priorities. We followed that decision with disciplines that accomplished each priority.

---

*Persistence is stubbornness
with a purpose.*

The Big Picture Frame
Big picture people
understand that commitment
is the journey
after the decision.

Without commitment, a beautiful wedding will not produce a lasting marriage. Likewise, without commitment, a glorious conversion will not produce genuine discipleship. Like a strong marriage, discipleship is the product of a relationship based upon renewing commitment daily.

Maximum Living

Rockingham, Georgia, in the 1940s and 1950s was a tiny village, located beside the railroad tracks about three miles east of Alma, the county seat. Alma was also small. A friend of mine said that Alma was "so small that their idea of heavy industry is a 300-pound Avon lady."

It was in that small town that I met the man who had a profound impact on my life. Rev. M. J. Wood was the pastor of the church we attended in Alma. When my dad passed away, this faithful servant of Christ stepped into my life and provided much of the guidance I desperately needed during my teen years. I especially remember his sermon titled "Living on the Extra Mile," based on Matt. 5:41. He dared us to reach beyond spiritual mediocrity and to experience Christ to the maximum. I can still hear his thundering voice today: "When will we become sick and tired of minimum Christian living and surrender ourselves so totally to Christ's control that we can experience His presence, purity, and power in our lives to the maximum?"

During his message I relived that fishing trip when my dad and I walked the footlog across the creek and refused to stop until we reached the better fishing hole. I remembered that there was no easy way or cleared path to the other side of the creek. I wondered why so few had ventured there.

Then Rev. Wood interrupted my reminiscing to conclude his message with an invitation: "You're invited to kneel at the altar, surrender fully to Christ, and allow Him to lead you into a new dimension of spiritual victory. There should be plenty of room at the altar this morning, because there are no traffic jams on the extra mile."

I knelt at the altar that morning. I vowed in my heart to know and experience Christ to the maximum. It started as a vision and a decision. As I allowed the life of Christ to overlay my life, the result was a growing oneness. I had no desire to be a dabbler. I determined to be a true disciple of Christ and began to live my life with the disciplines that daily affirmed my decision.

No Substitute

Commitment is the key to the life of the disciple. Nothing else substitutes for it—not promises, not enthusiasm, not even a try-harder mentality. Commitment is making the trip you mapped out. Commitment takes you down before it lifts you up. Commitment empties you before it fills you. Commitment is the life of discipleship. Nothing less will get you to the finish line.

Action Points

- ✓ Does Jesus describe my life as the fruit of His obedience?
- ✓ Am I holding on to anything that would prevent Christ from giving me His everything?
- ✓ Have I moved from vision, decision, and union to the daily discipline of living out my commitment to Christ?
- ✓ Is there anything I need to do today to affirm my commitment to live as a disciple of Jesus Christ?

Think About It

Most of us talk servanthood better than we practice it.

Motivation is dreams
that have put on work clothes.

*Do not merely listen to the word,
and so deceive yourselves. Do what it says.*
—James 1:22

13

Starting and Finishing

Before you can accomplish anything, you must start.

Nothing in life happens without a beginning. There is always a first step before a second. There is a starting line before a finish line. *Before you can accomplish anything, you must start.* It may sound simple, but it's vitally important. We attend seminars or read helpful books about ministry or the Christian life. We want to try all the great ideas, but months later we haven't followed through on any of them. Why not? Were the ideas not good enough? More likely we failed to seize one or two key ideas and set specific goals by which to implement them. Our intentions were good, but we failed to do anything with them. The old adage is too easy to prove: The road to failure is paved with good intentions.

Don't forget that the Christian journey is not a dash—it's a marathon! When we start the race, we determine to run faithfully and finish strong. We desire to keep the fire of His presence burning radiantly in our lives.

Unfortunately, the tendency of fire is to go out! Fire needs regular attention. We can't live on ashes from memories of what God did in our lives in the past. We have to add fuel to the fire every day. It's important to starting, and it's vital to finishing.

There are two ways to add fuel: with the Word and with the Spirit.

The Word

Jesus called the will of His Father His food. He told His disciples to pray for daily bread. He told a group of people who shared a miraculous picnic with Him that He was the living Bread. By the time John wrote his story of Jesus, he understood that Jesus was God's Word. There's no way around the fact that God's Word as He sent it to us through prophets and servants and Jesus represents something so basic to the Christian life that to live without it is to starve.

We must read His Word, hear His Word, and do His Word. We must treat it as important as food. If we start our day without it, we'll eventually experience an energy crisis. His Word is our fuel. We have no fire without it.

The Spirit

Just as we fan the beginning embers of a fire to get a flame started, the Holy Spirit is the wind that fans the flame of Christ's life in us. Without His daily filling, prompting, correcting, and counsel, we're dying embers. There's no way to produce the life of God without His Spirit fanning us with fresh wind to keep the fire flaming.

The problem is not that we don't know these things. The problem is that we don't set the goals and develop the disciplines that apply these truths. The problem is that too many think involvement in the Christian life is little more than starting. The problem is that too many have become spectators when Jesus invited them to be participants.

Spectator Versus Participant

Several years ago I attended a college football game in Athens, Georgia. Bear Bryant's Alabama Crimson Tide rolled over the Georgia Bulldogs. In the crowded parking lot after the game, I mused, "About 60,000 spectators, but only 22 participants." The Holy Spirit seemed to whisper, "A picture of the Church. For every 22 who put on the whole armor of God and faithfully fight the good fight of faith, there are 60,000 willing to sit safely in the bleachers and watch."

Are you a spectator or a participant?

Contrary to popular opinion, Christianity is not a spectator sport. Every believer is a minister! Everyone is involved.
—James L. Garlow

SPECTATORS	PARTICIPANTS
Spectators talk about problems.	Participants become problem solvers.
Spectators know the right answers.	Participants *live* the right answers.
Spectators think someone should teach, clean up, reach out to the community.	Participants ask God if they should teach, clean up, reach out to the community.
Spectators want to attend a "good church."	Participants understand that the church is as good as its participants.
Spectators worship to meet their needs.	Participants worship to meet God.

Not for Spectators

I was traveling a country road in western Pennsylvania when, in front of a small church, I saw a large sign that immediately captured my attention. It read, "Come to church tonight and watch the Holy Ghost perform."

As I continued down the winding back road, I couldn't stop thinking about that sign. It reinforced my opinion that we're obsessed with entertainment. Nothing demonstrates this more than the fact that professional athletes, movie stars, and rock musicians are the highest-paid individuals in our nation.

We even go to church to be entertained. If the choir, pastor, and other "performers" on the platform fail to entertain us, we find a different church with better "performers."

But worship is not something we watch. Instead, God is our audience, and we're the performers, every one of us, whether we're on the platform, in the choir loft, or in the congregation. "Worship" is an action verb. To worship, we must become *active* participants.

Worship is giving the best we have
unreservedly to God.
—Oswald Chambers

To live effectively and victoriously and make it to the finish line, you and I must discover *true* worship. There's only one way to do that. We must take time to focus on the greatness of God and His awesome grace. We must see Him as the God of creation and the God of redemption. We must see Him as the source of our physical life and our spiritual life.

A Lesson from a Potter

A trip one summer day to the Hopi Indian Reservation in northern Arizona reminded me in a powerful way of the greatness of our God. As I strolled with one of my Hopi friends through an ancient village perched on top of a mesa, he introduced me to a very old Hopi gentleman. For more than five decades, this gentleman had taken ordinary lumps of clay and transformed them into vessels of rare and exquisite beauty. But every place I looked as we walked along, I saw broken pieces of pottery. I was certain that the potter never intended that his work would become fragmented discards.

The First Potter

My thoughts turned to the Master Potter, the Creator God, who took just a handful of dirt and fashioned humanity. He left His fingerprints upon us and breathed His life into us, giving us spiritual life and moral accountability.

But there was an outlaw in God's universe! God's arch-enemy came to Adam and Eve and planted seeds of doubt by raising questions about His goodness, fairness, integrity, and sovereignty. Tragic rebellion, mutiny, and treason followed. The creature rejected the Creator and formed an alliance with Satan, God's ultimate enemy. The outlaw nature of Satan invaded the human heart. Every descendant of Adam became a sinful, broken, discarded vessel.

Repairing Broken Vessels

The Creator could have been finished with us. He had every right and reason to turn His back on the rebellious creatures who refused His guidance and spurned His love. But God's plan of redemption was already unfolding. The commandments, the covenants, the prophets, and the psalms point to a glorious day when the Redeemer would come. Then, one unforgettable day, John the Baptist shouted, "Behold! The Lamb of God who takes away the sin of the world!" (John 1:29, NKJV).

The spotless, worthy Lamb is lifted between earth and heaven. He spills His blood to purchase all the broken vessels of Adam's helpless race. In triumph, He declares, "It is finished" (John 19:30). Crushed, disjointed, discarded vessels can now be made whole by the power of the gospel of Jesus Christ! (Rom. 1:16).

We say that Jesus preached the gospel,
but He did more: He came
that there might be a gospel to preach.
—Oswald Chambers

Starting with God

The fact that God created us is good news. However, the fact He *redeemed* us is glorious news! How do we respond to this? First, we celebrate. Worship is gathering together to celebrate God's good news. It starts with what God did—not what we need. We worship the God who created us and redeemed us from the penalty, power, and pollution of sin's bondage. "Worship" is the word we use to describe acts of praise, adoration, honor, celebration, and obedience directed toward the God who sets us free—free to be who He designed us to be, to be cleaned vessels whom He fills with the Holy Spirit. We celebrate the mystery that Christ lives in us and through us. But worship isn't over when the pastor pronounces the benediction.

Worship Leads to Witness

When we discover true worship, our hearts will begin to burn with a passionate desire to make Christ known to others. Worship leads to witness. As Peter said, "We cannot help speaking about what we have seen and heard" (Acts 4:20).

If the average church would suddenly
take seriously the notion that every lay
member—man or woman—is really a
minister of Christ, we could have
something like a revolution in a
very short time.
—Elton Trueblood

When we leave the place of worship on Sunday, we enter our mission field. No disciple of Jesus Christ is without one. It's where we live, where we work, and where we play. God scatters His disciples on purpose. He wants people to come in contact with the gospel as they see it in His servants' lives. Are we faithful, consistent witnesses of the power of Jesus Christ to rescue and restore broken vessels?

What is 750,000 miles long,
reaches around the world 30 times,
and grows 20 miles longer each day?
The line of people without Christ.
— Pulpit Helps

It's Not Too Late—Yet!

Jesus pointed to fields ready for harvest and compared the whole world to a ready crop. That was 2,000 years ago. Today, people are as ready as ever to hear and respond to the gospel. Methods don't change the mission. Culture doesn't change our original condition. What will it take from you? A smile? A word? An act of kindness? For-

The Big Picture Frame

God so loved the world

that he gave his one and only Son,

that whoever believes in him

shall not perish but have eternal life.

—John 3:16

giveness? Gentleness? A new commitment? Whatever it takes, it's not as much as Jesus gave. Don't think about how big the mission is or how little one person can do. Think about who lives next door and how short the walk across the street is. Think about how much you have in God to share. Think about the big picture.

The hour is late. Let's get started.

Action Points

- ✓ What fuel do I depend on to keep my spiritual energy at its peak?
- ✓ Am I a spectator or a participant? In discipleship? Stewardship? Worship? Evangelism?
- ✓ Am I actively involved in sharing the Good News with someone who is a broken vessel?
- ✓ Has the Holy Spirit pointed out something He wants to address in my life?
- ✓ Am I ready to start working on it?

Think About It

The start is important,
but it's the finish
that counts.

Appendix

Recommended Reading

Bolin, Dan, and John Trent. *How to Be Your Wife's Best Friend.* Colorado Springs: Pinon Press, 1994.

Bushong, Burnis H. *The Best of the Story.* Marion, Ind.: World Gospel Mission, 1993.

Dillon, William R. *People Raising: A Practical Guide to Raising Support.* Chicago: Moody Press, 1993.

Duewel, Wesley. *Mighty Prevailing Prayer.* Grand Rapids: Zondervan Publishing House, 1990.

Elmore, Tim. *Mentoring: How to Invest Your Life in Others.* Atlanta: EQUIP, 1998.

Maxwell, John. *Developing the Leader Within You.* Nashville: Thomas Nelson Publishers, 1993.

———. *Developing the Leaders Around You.* Nashville: Thomas Nelson Publishers, 1995.

———. *Leadership 101.* Tulsa, Okla.: Honor Books, 1994.

———. *Partners in Prayer.* Nashville: Thomas Nelson Publishers, 1996.

Piper, John. *Let the Nations Be Glad.* Grand Rapids: Baker Book House, 1993.

Sanders, J. Oswald. *Spiritual Leadership.* Chicago: Moody Press, 1994.

Telford, John. *Sayings and Portraits of John Wesley.* Salem, Ohio: Schmul Publishing, 1995.

Toler, Stan. *God Has Never Failed Me, but He Has Sure Scared Me to Death a Few Times.* Tulsa, Okla.: Honor Books, 1995.

Toler, Stan, and Elmer Towns. *Developing a Giving Church.* Kansas City: Beacon Hill Press of Kansas City, 1999.

EQUIP

EQUIP is a not-for-profit Christian organization whose letters stand for "Encouraging Qualities Undeveloped In People." Founded in 1996 by John C. Maxwell, the organization provides a unique global partnering network focused to develop Great Commission leaders. EQUIP provides leadership training and resources for leaders in the least evangelized nations, in America's urban communities, and on high school, college, and seminary campuses.

More information is available by contacting the group.

DATE DUE
